THE BASKETBALL COACH

GUIDES TO SUCCESS

John W. Bunn

BASKETBALL COACH
COLORADO STATE COLLEGE
GREELEY, COLORADO

PRENTICE-HALL, INC.   Englewood Cliffs, N.J.   1961

D1455731

PREFACE

Basketball has become such a highly organized business that the fringe areas of the game tend to overshadow the technical features incidental to play. In other words, the more important job of the coach seems to center around the duties of recruiting, promotion, public relations, salesmanship, and organization. Less and less emphasis and attention is devoted to coaching the techniques of play. At least, the former group of responsibilities has enlarged so that more and more time is required of the coach, thereby distracting him from his players and from their personal basketball needs.

The Basketball Coach: Guides to Success, which treats of the by-products of the game, is the first of two volumes. The second volume deals entirely with playing techniques, drills to perfect player habit patterns, and team organization for both offensive and defensive tactics. This division of materials permits a more thorough treatment in both cases, and the proper emphasis can be given to each part without detracting from the importance of either. At the same time, one volume ably supplements the other. Together, the two volumes provide a complete treatise on basketball.

An attempt has been made not only to bring up to date the sum of the experiences and knowledge of the author since his first publication, "Basketball Methods," but also to report the more pertinent research now available. Many fallacious opinions can now be replaced by fact. The present-day coach can be much more certain than was his predecessor of his plans of procedure if he provides himself with current materials.

In return for the invaluable assistance he has received from them, the author wishes to share his experience with his colleagues. This book is, in a sense, a "thank you" and a wish for good luck.

JOHN W. BUNN

TABLE OF CONTENTS

v

BASKETBALL—
AN INTRODUCTION

Basketball is unique in the annals of sports. It was created out of dire necessity—the need to provide a challenging, vigorous, competitive activity that could be played indoors and to satisfy a rebellious group of football players (future YMCA secretaries) who were eagerly waiting until a New England winter would subside so they could get outside for spring baseball. It seemed almost prophetic that a man with vision, imagination, and ingenuity should be on the scene to meet the need.

This was the setting that faced Dr. James Naismith, a graduate student at Springfield College in Massachusetts, in 1891. How well he met the need is attested to by the fact that basketball is the greatest game we have today—played and witnessed by more people than baseball and football combined. How great was his vision is evidenced by the fact that the thirteen original rules are basically the same now—no running; no charging, tackling, or holding; no hitting the ball with the fist; penalties for rules violations; and an elevated horizontal goal. His ingenuity is shown by his choice of goal. He wanted a box but accepted peach baskets which the janitor had available. By elevating the goals above the floor he provided the challenge which gave eternal life to the game. Never before had there been a game with the goals elevated above the playing surface and placed horizontally instead of vertically. The first impulse to old and young alike as they pick up a basketball is to look up at the goal and wonder, "Can I put it through the hoop?"

The game flourished from the beginning, and was played by women as readily as by men. It spread to foreign countries as soon as it was played in different parts of the United States. The rugged secretaries introduced it wherever they went, and it even became a problem in some localities because it was crowding out other activities. At one time there was a threat to ban its use in YMCA programs.

Naismith left Springfield for the University of Kansas and took the game with him. Although Springfield College is the birthplace of basketball, Kansas is its cradle. It was there that Phog Allen came under the tutelage of Naismith and became probably the first professional coach when he took a job at Baker University in Baldwin, Kansas. Before he completed his coaching career, he compiled the most outstanding record and greatest number of years of service of any coach in the world.

It was at Kansas that I met Naismith, that great humanitarian. He epitomized all the high idealism exemplified through sport. He was a kindly, humble, generous, understanding, Christian teacher, dedicated to the betterment of mankind. He was a licensed physician and an ordained minister, and these disciplines supplemented ideally his professional career in physical education. His interest was in people, his aim was to help them, and his brain-child, basketball, was an outcome of the drive of these qualities. Although he never exploited the game for his own gain, others profited tremendously. It is, therefore, fitting and proper that his benefactors should honor him by erecting a Basketball Hall of Fame on the campus at Springfield College, where the history and development of basketball may be accumulated and displayed. This structure, and its contents, are in continuous growth and stand as an invitation to all the world to give for its continued progress.

A few highlights of the game in its electric climb to world-wide acclaim are chronicled here to orient the reader:

1. The first rules were contained on two sheets of 8½ by 11 inch paper and were posted on the bulletin board in the gym at Springfield College. There were then thirteen rules. Now the rules cover forty pages. The number of rules have been reduced to ten, but these ten rules are divided into 97 sections and many notes, penalties, explanatory questions and answers, and interpretive comments. In addition, a book of interpretations containing approximately five hundred play situations is published each year.

The rules were first published at Springfield College and appeared in the *Triangle* of that institution. As the game spread to schools and clubs and grew in popularity, a National Rules Committee was formed, with representatives from various interested groups. At one time separate sets of rules were adopted and published by the A.A.U., the colleges, the high schools, and the YMCA; but the infeasibility of the many variations of more than one set of rules was soon realized. Now there is a National Basketball Committee of the United States and Canada which adopts a uniform set of rules for all amateur organizations in the United States and Canada. This organization meets annually to consider changes in the rules.

The professional teams have a different set of rules; and the Federation of International Basketball Associations, to which nearly a hundred countries belong, publishes a set of rules different from all others. These rules are used for international play and for Olympic competition. This organization considers rules legislation once every four years, at the time of the Olympic games.

2. Dr. Forrest C. Allen became probably the first professional basketball coach when in 1904 he accepted an invitation to coach the Baker University team at Baldwin, Kansas. When Dr. Naismith heard of his appointment, he remarked to him: "Why, Phog, you don't coach basketball, you just play it!"

Dr. Allen's early contribution to the game was the development of sound fundamentals based upon scientific principles of kinesiology and mechanics, and his exploitation of the zone defense. Allen organized a team of his brothers and toured the country in the early days. The Allen boys' team was as famous as the Buffalo Germans and the original Celtics. Allen's books, *My Basketball Bible* and *Better Basketball,* were standbys for all coaches.

There are other great coaches who were pioneers in the game. Hager was noted for his "percentage basketball," and his book by this title described his system of play. Dr. Walter Meanwell was noted for his precision play, and his book, *Science of Basketball for Men,* was a guide in the early days. He and Dr. Allen were great rivals. He was as much an institution at the University of Wisconsin and Missouri as was Dr. Allen at the University of Kansas.

Ralph Jones, the pioneer of the fast break, wrote one of the early books, *Basketball for Coaches and Players.* He, Allen, and Meanwell would be considered the big three in early-day basketball. His influence was particularly felt in the Big Ten area.

Nat Holman, one of the original Celtics, introduced the professional style of the game to amateur basketball. His "single post" and "give and go" techniques were characteristic of all basketball on the Atlantic Coast for many years. Most of his coaching career was spent at the City College of New York.

Dr. H. C. Carlson, associated with the University of Pittsburgh, contributed the idea of continuity, which is characteristic of modern-day basketball.

3. Amos Alonzo Stagg, who is generally remembered in connection with football, probably made his greatest contribution to basketball. He played on the first basketball team of Springfield College.

While at the University of Chicago, he organized and conducted the National High School Basketball Tournament, which was the first national tournament of its kind. This tournament started in 1917 and was stopped in 1929, when the National Federation of State High School Athletic Associations dis-

couraged intersectional games, overemphasis, and long absences
of high school students from school. The tournament was also
being exploited by college coaches for recruiting basketball
talent.

4. The National Association of Basketball Coaches was
organized in 1926 to protest the elimination of the dribble by the
rules committee. So powerful was the influence of its twenty-
one charter members that the rules committee rescinded its
action before the change could be put into print. Dr. Forrest C.
Allen was the initiating force in the formation of this body and
served as its first president. The organization has continued its
strong leadership in basketball and has been directly responsible
for much of the progress of college basketball.

5. Basketball became an Olympic sport in 1936 when the
games were held in Berlin. Dr. Allen was largely responsible
for the acceptance of basketball as an Olympic event. His untiring efforts were rewarded after five years of aggressive effort.
Now, a Federation of International Basketball Associations,
organized in 1932, promotes and controls basketball throughout
the world and adopts the rules for Olympic play. Its head-
quarters are in Geneva, Switzerland and its membership included
eighty-seven countries in 1960.

6. Dr. and Mrs. Naismith were sent to the first Olympic
Basketball Games as guests of the National Association of
Basketball Coaches. This act led to a desire to honor further
the inventor of the game. The creation of the Basketball Hall
of Fame at Springfield College was the result. The project was
promoted by the Coaches Association and is a memorial to Dr.
Naismith.

7. In 1939 the National Association of Basketball Coaches
organized the first National Collegiate Basketball Tournament.
The University of Oregon, with Howard Hobson as coach,
produced the first national champion. The first finals were
played at Northwestern University in Evanston, Illinois, with
Harold Olson of Ohio State University as chairman of the committee which handled this event.

The tournament is now administered by the NCAA. Revenue from this tournament furnishes the main source of funds by means of which the NCAA carries on its activities.

8. Basketball has experienced many changes, but two stand out most prominently. The first is in the character of the game. The elimination of the center jump, the development and perfection of techniques, particularly the jump shot, and the advent of the tall player have changed the game from a comparatively slow, low-scoring contest into a fast, exciting, high-scoring event. This change has catapulted the game to the forefront as the greatest spectator contest and the team sport played by the greatest number of people.

Second, the game is gradually turning into a professional event at the colleges and universities. It is big business. High school graduates with basketball talent are solicited and bid for intensively. They are literally paid to attend college to play basketball. Their pseudo-amateur standing is dignified by sanctioned rules. Such rules, however, do not change the untarnished fact that actually this is professionalism; and the trend intended to control and regularize recruiting and subsidization may well defeat its own purpose. This is the only blot on an otherwise glorious picture of the progress of the greatest game on earth.

1

A COACHING
PHILOSOPHY

Webster defines philosophy as "A systematic body of general conceptions or principles ordinarily with implications of their practical application." Everyone has a philosophy. Every basketball coach has a basketball philosophy. That philosophy reflects his attitude toward boys and toward the sport, and it dictates the kind of game he will coach.

The purpose of this chapter is to present a philosophy of coaching which relates sports to education and life and forms the only justifiable basis for including sports in an educational program. (In a sense, this chapter becomes a preview of all that is to follow in the succeeding chapters and in the second volume.) Implicit in this philosophy is the thesis that sports provide the only practical laboratory for all aspects of education and life. And, since sports are so dynamic and challenging, they reveal the individual participant in his true light.

SPORTS—AN INTEGRAL PART
OF EDUCATION

In the first place, sports (in this instance basketball), if they are to be included in the school program, should be an integral

7

part of the total educational program; they should receive neither more nor less support than any other area of the curriculum. Teams should be made up of students who, on their own initiative, desire to participate. There should be no more solicitation of athletes than of any other students, nor should there be any inducements or awards other than those available to other students. Sports should be conducted for the benefit of and in the interests of the students and not at their expense or for their exploitation. The sports program should be financed and administered in the same way as other aspects of the educational program. In short, a sports program in an educational institution is difficult to justify when conducted on any basis other than as an integral part of the educational program. Unfortunately, too many sports programs would not be recognized by these characteristics. But, there are many institutions which operate according to the above plan; and most secondary schools have a truly educational program.

The methods practiced in interschool sports provide the pattern upon which the total program for physical education should be based. In an age of soft living, the vigorous, intense nature of interschool sports is the only sound basis upon which to build the physical education program for the total student body. Fitness for emergencies, for survival, and for healthful living cannot be attained by other methods, certainly not by passive activities.

THE INFLUENCE OF THE COACH

The coach is the key to the benefits that will accrue to the players as a result of their participation in the sport. He wields a powerful influence over his players. In order to get to play, they will submit to almost any demand he may make of them. They reflect their coach regardless of his principles, and the institution is measured by the kind of man he is.

Recently, one of the most admirable leaders in basketball resigned his coaching job in one of our great universities under the pressure of not having won a championship. Yet, the constructive and positive influence which he has had on his boys is worth more than a hundred championships. The respect and esteem with which he is held by his colleagues has reflected his institution in a most favorable light. His successor may win more games with his teams, but the institution which places winning ahead of constructive leadership is bound to suffer in retrospect.

BE YOURSELF

A coach, to do his best job, must be himself. He cannot be a shadow of another. Personalities and backgrounds are never the same. They may be antithetic. One person is phlegmatic, another high-strung; one is mild-mannered, another hard-driving and demanding; one may be kind and personal, another cruel, even brutal; one may be encouraging and complimentary, another discouragingly critical. A coach may have a basketball hero (his old coach, for instance) whom he idealizes, but he should not try to mimic him. A coach should study the performance (which is the implementation of a philosophy) of all his colleagues and predecessors. From such a study, he may find valuable and useful ideas which he can incorporate into his own philosophy. He should, however, pick and choose on the basis of whether or not the principles of others fit his own to help make a more effective and harmonious whole. To sum up, "To thine own self be true"—be yourself.

COACH-PLAYER RELATIONSHIPS

Coach-player relationships should be such that a lasting, wholesome influence is created. A coach may be stern, dignified, and formal; he may be cordial, personal, and informal as befits his own characteristics. But if his relationship with his players is to be worthwhile, he must command their respect not only at the time they are playing, but more particularly after ten years have elapsed. This should be true in defeat as well as in victory. They should respect him as a man as well as a coach.

To earn this kind of relationship, the coach must be a person of high standards. He must be a desirable example for his boys. He must be ready to defend them when they are maligned. He must demand of them the highest integrity and not be reluctant to discipline them when such methods are indicated. And yet, he must have a forgiving heart without being weak and vacillating. He must recognize that he is being entrusted with boys who are growing to be men; boys who, in the process, are often groping and need a friendly guiding hand of one who is a bit farther along the road.

THE GAME SHOULD BE FUN

Baskebtall should be fun for those who play and for those who coach the game. This does not mean there is no hard work to gain perfection, no strenuous effort to attain top condition, or no self-denial in the interests of the team. In the last analysis, these help to make the game more enjoyable. Even these arduous preparatory tactics can be great fun if an enthusiastic attitude is created toward them. I actually believe there is more enthusiastic spirit generated for the very intense conditioning exercises which my teams go through each pre-season than there is for any other stage of our practice. The players have learned that gaining top condition permits them to play with zest throughout a game and throughout the season, so they make fun of what could be drudgery. There is more bantering, kidding, and whooping-it-up than at any other time during practice.

Every red-blooded American plays hard to win. But, when players are sorry to see a strenuous season come to a close whether they have been winning or losing, it is a sure sign that they have been having fun. The coach, by his attitude and his emphasis, can help build this kind of spirit within his squad.

To have fun does not imply a lack of serious effort. It does, however, indicate a lack of tenseness. It indicates a state of relaxation which is necessary to the best in basketball performance, because a tense, worried, harried team is not likely to perform at its best. The author has worried more when his team appeared too tense. He has resorted to more tactics to produce relaxation than to create a serious attitude.

Often, incidental acts create the desired mental poise when planned tactics are ineffective. The first championship play-off in which the author's team, a sophomore group, participated is a case in point. Before the game, the squad was too serious and so tense and irritable that it was not pleasant to be around. Planned attempts to change the atmosphere were futile. But a chance prank turned the trick and sent a carefree squad on the floor to win easily over a team which had soundly defeated it twice, earlier in the season.

The first appearance of the author's squad in Madison Square Garden was another example. The team started the game under great tension and was not playing up to its ability. Midway during the first half a player in control of the ball fell at the free-throw line. As he fell he tossed the ball back over his head. By some stroke of luck, the ball went through the basket in a perfect arch. The player who tossed the ball stood in amazement when told by this teammates that he had scored a goal. This crazy incident caused the whole squad to break into uproarious laughter. What was previously a nip-and-tuck game turned into a rout of the top team of the East and created the monicker of "the laughing boys" for the team.

These illustrations can be multiplied. These two, however, are sufficient to emphasize the fact that for the best interests of the boys and the best results, one should play to win, but have fun in doing it.

PRACTICE DEMOCRACY

Democratic policies should be practiced with the squad. Democracy implies leading and following. It also means that all should have a voice in making decisions. It is recognized that the coach has certain definite responsibilities thrust upon him; however, much value can come out of sharing with the players. Plans of play strategies can be presented and the opinion of the squad secured. Many times, excellent suggestions come from squad members; and when they are brought into the picture in this manner, players feel as though they have a more important part to play and it builds greater unity in the squad.

To permit the squad to select its own captain, or floor leader, is more democratic than for the coach to appoint him. This is another means of building greater unity in a squad—permitting the boys to exercise their own choice. One need not fear clique action if the coach has established desirable coach-player relations. The boys usually give stronger support to their own leader than they are likely to give to a leader imposed upon them. In most instances, the players choose the boy with the best leadership qualities. They sense who the leaders are.

Unfortunately, the social trend in America has been to stifle democratic principles. In sport, we should do everything possible to nurture them.

ENCOURAGE FREEDOM AND INITIATIVE

Akin to democratic action is the encouragement of freedom and initiative in play. Play should not be so mechanized in its organization that no freedom of choice is left to the players. Basketball action changes so much during the progress of a game that it is detrimental for a team to be too stereotyped in its play. It is impossible for the coach to plan every move in advance; therefore, practice and organization of play should be set up so that the players are encouraged to think and are given an opportunity to use their own initiative. A team organized on this plan is always more resourceful. When unusual situations arise, they are usually able to cope with them successfully.

The author has always developed a general plan of offensive movement for his team with the definite provision that the player with the ball is free to do whatever seems best to him under the circumstances at that moment. On defense the primary goal is to get the ball. The players are free to use any tactics which they feel will help them to get the ball. What better method is there to develop freedom and initiative in American youth?

ENCOURAGE FAST AND AGGRESSIVE PLAY

A fast and aggressive game should be taught. Contrary to the opinion of many coaches, there is as much plan and organization in a fast-break, passing type of game as there is in a conservative, ball-control game. The fast, aggressive game is more difficult to learn, but there are several reasons for advocating this type of play. It permits greater freedom and more initiative. It is more fun. Players generally like a fast, aggressive style of play. It is consistent with the foregoing phases of our philosophy. In addition, it is better strategy to prepare a team to play fast. A fast team can play a slow game, but a slow team has great difficulty adjusting to a fast game.

Bob Richards, the great Olympic pole vaulter, has said that sports symbolize life situations. The important thing is to provide an atmosphere in which, by the way boys react to the challenges they receive in sports, they are strengthened for their role as responsible citizens. The coaching philosophy which has just been described is directed toward that goal. It is the author's philosophy.

2

THE COACH

This chapter is written with a twofold purpose. It is intended first of all to show to coaches and to aspiring coaches the exalted positions they occupy. It is intended as a challenge to them to measure up to the responsibility which they assume and to grasp the opportunity which is before them.

In the second place it is directed to administrators. It is intended as a guide in the selection of one to assume the duties of a coach. It is written with the conviction that there are qualifications prerequisite to the position of coach which need not be present in other teaching positions.

RESPONSIBILITY OF THE COACH

The coach occupies a position of tremendous responsibility and influence. Because of the great appeal which athletic compeion has for young people in America, they will meet any requirement and undergo any restrictions and hardships in order to qualify for competition or for a place on a team. As a consequence, the coach has a golden opportunity to mold the practical aspects of the lives of those who come under his tutelage—their habits, their character, their health, their attitudes, their general development. Because of the close personal relationship he inevitably maintains with the members of his team—a relationship not common to other teachers and in many cases not even present between parents and their children—a coach cannot avoid having a high degree of influence upon them.

It is characteristic of youngsters to be hero worshipers. The coach is the hero to his players. Whatever he does and whatever he asks his players to do is accepted without question. He is emulated by his followers, and his methods and his acts, even though they may be unsound and have a negative influence, are still accepted as standards. The common argument and conception that sports in themselves will develop and bring out only the good qualities in an individual will not survive objective and impersonal analysis. Competition will bring to the surface in bold relief the caliber of an individual. The intensity of competitive athletics brings out one's qualities unconsciously. They can be just as bad as they are good. All depends upon the quality of the leader, the coach. This fact points to the necessity for not only a thorough training but also a wide training for the prospective coach. It demands further that only those of impeccable character should be chosen if positive results are to be obtained. On the basis of this introduction, the following qualifications for a coach are discussed.

MORAL INTEGRITY

The first consideration is that of moral excellence. This is a quality that is not always revealed during an interview. It is not necessarily what one says but rather how one lives that shows the mark of a man. The slogan, "It is better to lead by example than by edict," although true in all cases, is absolutely necessary for a coach if the most positive results are to be attained. As a consequence, an exhaustive inquiry should be made concerning the habits and conduct of a prospective coach. This can be determined through recommendations, through a record of previous experiences, and from personal inquiry. The last method is probably the most reliable. Recommendations must be scrutinized carefully. Those solicited or presented by the coach are more often from persons who may not be objective or impersonal in their evaluation. Those from teachers are usually most reliable. A good general criterion to use in measuring moral integrity is to ask, "Is this the type of man I would be glad to have in charge of my son?"

If one desires the highest qualities of sportmanship developed, then he should be sure that the leader has these qualities. If one is interested in the quality of clean speech, then the coach cannot set an example of blasphemy and smut. If gentlemanly conduct is to be developed, the coach should be a gentleman. Moreover, it is equally important to have strongly exemplified in the coach the qualities of respect for others and of honesty and trustworthiness, for the salutary effect they may have upon the players.

ABILITY TO TEACH

The second characteristic of the coach is a measure of his ability to teach. This characteristic includes the ability to lead. All the information available on basketball is of little value unless one has the knack of imparting that information to another so that he can convert it into effective action. Not only must one teach at the level of understanding of his squad, but he must also present his material in a logical sequence and in an inspiring manner so that the players will be highly motivated to action. The effective application of the laws of learning is necessary if the squad is to approach the level of its potential. It is not enough merely to cover the subject matter as is the usual procedure in the classroom. The squad must be drilled and drilled and drilled (the law of repetition) until everyone becomes automatic in his performance of patterns and techniques. Sometimes the effort seems useless, but the coach who is dedicated to his boys never gives up.

Several years ago a coach worked for three years with a boy on a particular maneuver, but the boy did not seem to be able to acquire the skill. Then one day in scrimmage he caught on and played brilliantly. His coach complimented him enthusiastically on his play. The boy beamed and then said, "Coach, I just discovered something." He then proceeded to describe in minute detail the technique which the coach had labored to teach him. He had made the discovery "on his own initiative." We can never know when our teaching will finally penetrate. As F. C. Allen once said, "repeat four thousand nine hundred and ninety-nine times and then once more." The goal is to develop all to the level of an "A" student. The results of teaching are on public display regularly. There is no consolation in complaining about the caliber of a candidate and to flunk him if he does not measure up to an absolute standard. The coach, unlike the classroom teacher, flunks with him. The job is, "Whatsoever thy hand findeth to do, do it with thy might." Probably no one ever reaches the limit of his potentiality. The job then is to use every possible teaching device at one's command toward helping each boy to rise to heights undreamed of. If by this means a will to achieve is created, the results will be most surprising and gratifying both to the player and to his coach.

Implicit in the ability to teach is the ability to lead: to lead youngsters toward the attainment of high standards and toward becoming respectable citizens, to demand the best and not to accept anything less. Sometimes one takes great criticism for holding to his standards; but in the end he is always highly respected, often by those who were his severest critics. Players seldom respect a coach who does not have the courage to stick by the standards which he sets for his squad. But they will support him loyally when he has the courage, even in the face of disaster, to act in accordance with the code for the squad.

Jim Baggott, whose high school teams have made history for years and whose teams have gone to the state tournament in Colorado more years in succession than any other triple A team in the state, once had the unpleasant task of dismissing four of his first five players from the squad on the eve of going to the state tournament. This act so inspired the other members of the squad that they won the state tournament anyway. The boys who were disciplined are now the coach's most ardent supporters. They were awakened by his courage and they respect him for the help he gave them.

PREPARATION OF THE COACH

Third, every coach should have a background in the basic courses of the curriculum in physical education. These include psychology, biology, physiology, anatomy, kinesiology, physiology of exercise, health education, and first aid.

A coach is responsible for the health and safety of his boys. A successful leader thinks of the welfare of his followers first and always provides for their needs. How can a coach know how to train and condition a squad intelligently, know their limitations, be able to protect them from dangerous action, and care for them in emergencies unless he has a background of training to guide him in his decisions? No one should be entrusted with a group of boys in athletic competition who is not trained with the basic knowledge of his profession. No wise individual would select a physician who is not thoroughly trained for his profession. As a matter of fact, state laws will certify no one for the practice of medicine unless he is adequately trained.

Too often a coach is chosen because he was a great player. Such a choice may beget some initial publicity for the school or the community, but unless the candidate has the qualifications for the job the choice may be a most disastrous one for the ultimate good of the community and the boys who are subjected to his leadership. Certainly, to be a great performer is not a recommendation per se. Unfortunately some boards of education in this enlightened age still succumb to the glamour of the star athlete.

Many institutions give minors in physical education as an attraction for boys who are interested in coaching. Too many of these courses are pure makeshifts. They fail to provide the basic requirements. Yet, the National Education Association recommends that even the minor in physical education should fulfill these requirements. The mere fact that one has a minor in physical education does not necessarily mean that he has the basic requirements for his profession. Therefore, investigation of the candidate should go deeper than the surface. Does he have the basic courses that make him a safe person to entrust with young boys in athletic competition?

Certainly, it is expected that he will have a knowledge of the sport he is to coach. This may be gained partially through competition, but seldom is a person thoroughly trained in all the techniques of a sport by playing. There is so much specialization these days that a thorough coverage of a sport can be gained only through a coaching methods course plus a theory and practice course in all the techniques of the activity. In addition, one needs constantly to refresh himself with the developments in his specialty through the current literature and coaching clinics that are given at schools all over the country during the summer. It is the wise coach who is always alert for new ideas, is critical of all theories, and demands scientific proof of the efficiency of all techniques.

THE COACH AS A COUNSELOR

Finally, one who would be a coach should include in his plan of study some courses in guidance and counseling. No one in the whole school system has a greater opportunity to advise students than the coach. Because of his close personal relationship with students and because of the informal basis upon which he meets them, he is taken into the confidence of the student more than any other member of the faculty. He seems to be accepted as one of them.

At a high school banquet, a student was introducing the members of the faculty who were present. He introduced each as Miss or Mr. So-and-So until he got to his coach whom he called by his first name. He realized what he had done, started to correct himself and then unabashedly said, "No, that's exactly what I mean. He seems more like one of us."

Because the coach is sought out in this way by students, he should prepare himself so that he may work intelligently with them and with the regular counseling agencies in his institution in the best interests of the students. The coach must be a master teacher in its true sense if he is to fulfill all his responsibilities and avail himself of his opportunities.

3

PUBLIC RELATIONS

Coaches are in the public eye more than any other member of the staff of an institution. They cannot avoid the limelight. Sports is a universal means of communication, and as a consequence, coaches of sports teams are placed in the center of a mad whirl. They are prominently on display during the course of a contest. They are continually asked to address civic, church, social, and school groups. They appear regularly for interviews and talks on radio and television. They are quoted constantly in the public press. They are the subject of praise and/or condemnation by the sports-loving public. Crises are created because of coaches and their teams, because of what they say, how they act, where they go, and what they do.

Whether or not this attention and notoriety constitute over-emphasis and are out of proportion to the importance of the individual and the activity is beside the point. The reality of the situation must be faced. The coach becomes a tremendous force for public relations, and as a consequence he carries a tremen-dous responsibility. His actions and comments must be weighed in terms of the institution which he represents rather than in terms of his own personal thoughts and feelings. He reflects his institution as well as himself, and he can be a tremendous force for good or a damaging influence.

PURPOSE

The purpose of this chapter is to discuss briefly procedures which the coach may follow in developing effective public relations for his institution and for his sport. Public relations in basketball consists of describing, interpreting, and relating the policies, philosophies, programs, trends, objectives, and values of the sport to the individual and the community. It is intended to build good will, lift the morale, create a favorable response, gain support and following, and, through these contributions, to serve better and influence more positively the institution and the community. It is a continuing program from hour to hour, day to day, and year to year.

Sports, particularly basketball, are most convenient media for developing public relations in a community for the whole school program. Because of the universal interest in and appeal of sports, they are being used effectively as a means of cultivating friendship and understanding between peoples of different nations. The promotion of the Olympic, Pan-American, Asiatic, European, and inter-military competitions are examples. Private, cultural, and social agencies are using coaches and teams in increasing numbers as a means of cultivating better relations with foreign countries and assisting them in developing their sports cultures. The author has participated in some of these programs and has been able to observe firsthand the tremendous impact of the programs.

PLACE OF COACH

The place of the coach is of first importance in any program of public relations. He must be the catalytic agent. He is the source of information for his sport. By his example, he sets the tone for the type of relationship which may be developed. His players reflect him at all times. His initiative and imagination will determine the extent and success of efforts to develop a public relations program. He should acquaint himself thoroughly with the policies of his institution and the philosophy of those who set these policies so that his actions and statements will be in harmony with these policies and philosophies.

If the opportunity is presented, the coach should associate himself with a civic organization. Such organizations provide a sounding board for him. They afford him an opportunity for invaluable contacts as well as provide a means for him to serve his community.

The tone of the publicity regarding his sport and his squad can be influenced by the manner in which the coach co-operates with the local sports writers. Most newspapermen have writing ability. Only a few are expert in their knowledge and understanding of sports. The coach can be very helpful to these men in the promotion of his sport if he will share with them his experiences, sport information, and analyses.

THE COACH—
A RESOURCE FOR FACTS

Much of the adverse publicity about basketball is based upon erroneous impressions and observations due to a lack of facts about the sport. Coaches should keep abreast of the trends and developments in their sport. They should collect and study statistics in order to have ready facts to present concerning the controversial issues, and by this means replace bias and misunderstanding with objective data.

Examples are legion. If it were known that free throws are no greater percentage of the total score of a game today than they were ten years ago, that the number of personal fouls today are fewer than they were ten years ago, and that approximately one-third of all games are won or lost because of free throws—the same percentage as ten years ago—there would not be the wild and critical statements that the game is nothing but a parade to the free-throw line. If it were known that the basketball in high school and college games is held on the average no longer than seven seconds before a shot or loss of team control occurs, that less than one per cent of the time is the ball held longer than thirty seconds before a shot or loss of control, that promiscuous and deliberate fouling was the primary reason for the time limit rule in professional basketball, that there is not the same balance in personnel and skill in high school and college basketball as there is in professional basketball, there would not be the tendency toward invidious comparisons. An informed public is usually a reasonable public.

THE HERITAGE OF BASKETBALL

Basketball has a great heritage. The ideals of the man who invented the game; the niche the game fills in the world of sport; the ease with which it fits into the recreation program for men and women of all ages; its adaptability for recreation purposes; the fact that more people play it and watch it than any other game; that it is more widespread internationally than any other sport in spite of the fact that it is our youngest game; that it has a very high rating as an activity for building fitness; and that it has equal value with other sports as a vehicle for developing good will and courageous, honorable, effective citizenship place basketball at the forefront of all our competitive team games. Nor should the fact be overlooked that basketball is the major source of financial support for the governing bodies for our athletic programs. The NCAA, the A.A.U., the NAIA, and the state high school associations depend on receipts from basketball for the expanded programs of these organizations in the interest of all sports.

KEEPING THE PUBLIC ABREAST OF TRENDS

Information concerning the rules, their interpretation, the principles of rulemaking, and the art of officiating will help the public to a better understanding and appreciation of the game;

it will also create a greater respect for the work of the officials. Much criticism and dissatisfaction with the administration of the game is due to a lack of understanding. The rules of the game are so simple that it is taken for granted that all know and understand them, but this is not the case. Television, radio, and the press can be utilized to correct this situation. Regular weekly quiz programs, demonstrations, planned interviews, and factual newspaper stories can be very informative.

The development of techniques, the organization of offense and defense, the use of strategic and psychological tactics have progressed beyond the knowledge of the average spectator. The coach can do much to keep the public apace with these advancements by presentations designed for popular consumption by the various organizations in his community. With increased understanding, the interest of these groups for the sport is much enhanced.

THE COACH AND THE FACULTY

In the interest of the general public, the need for good public relations with the school staff should not be overlooked. Many times those with whom one works are inadvertently taken for granted or ignored. Such an attitude can be misunderstood and can create or develop ill will or opposition. Moreover, the inordinate amount of publicity that the sports program receives can be a cause of jealousy on the part of staff members in other departments of the school.

The coach must be sensitive to these possibilities, and he should take steps to avoid them. In the first place, he should be certain that his colleagues are aware of his philosophy of sports. He should demonstrate by his practice that sports are an integral part of the total school program and that he recognizes the equal importance of the work of other departments. He should show a willingness and a desire to cooperate in the total school program and he should convince his colleagues that their interest and participation in the sports program is equally important.

TOTAL SCHOOL PARTICIPATION

Participation in basketball includes many people other than actual players. The program should be planned to provide activity for as many others as possible. By expanding it in this manner, stronger ties with the total community are welded. The managerial system should be fully expanded, and the cheerleaders and rooters organization as well as the band should be made an integral part of the program; these groups are very essential and valuable additions to the basketball family. A between-halves program which is varied from game to game is a clever means of introducing the programs and activities of other groups of the school and community and of associating them with basketball. Marching tactics, musical features, stunts, baton exhibitions, and gymnastic performances are special events to stir one's imagination.

THE PLACE OF THE
PUBLIC ADDRESS SYSTEM

The person in charge of the public address system can make a most valuable contribution to better public relations. Through the use of the public address, much can be done to control crowd behavior and set the tone for the whole program. In order to make a contribution to public relations, the public address must be used primarily as a source of information for the audience. Announcements and comments should be dignified, impersonal, courteous, objective, and always calm and controlled. The public address should be used with discretion. Continuous comment becomes irritable and objectionable. The announcer should not try to be an entertainer, and certainly he should not be a cheerleader. The audience should not be exploited through forced advertising of all the impending events on the calendar. The public address must be used for emergencies, of course, but certainly not to ask Mr. X to meet Miss Y in the lobby after the game. It is not a dating bureau. The public address system must be thought of in terms of serving the total audience and not specific individuals.

Great care must be taken to be fair to the visitors and not to reflect upon the work of the officials. Nicknames and first names of the home team should not be used unless the same information is available concerning the visitors. If personal items about the players of one team are used, similar information should be announced about the opponents. No comments of any kind should be made on the decisions of the officials. Right or wrong, their judgments are official and final and should be accepted without question.

An explanation of rules, perhaps not known or understood by the audience, upon which decisions are made is desirable and helpful to a better understanding of the game. For example, if the game for some reason or other is started by a free throw rather than by a jump ball, it is enlightening to announce the reason. A review of new rules at the early-season games is decidedly in the interest of the spectators and their better enjoyment of the game.

IMPORTANCE OF
SCORERS AND TIMERS

Scorers and timers should be chosen with the greatest care. Few realize that the records and decisions of the scorers and timers are final in the absence of any additional or contrary information on the part of the referee. Scorers and timers are therefore tremendously important to the game. They must be responsible, reliable individuals who are intimately acquainted with the rules pertaining to their jobs. They must be impersonal and objective and alert at all times. They cannot afford to become concerned to the point of bias, or emotionally involved in the outcome of the game.

In many respects they are equal to the referee and umpire in their importance to the game. It is a great relief to the referee and umpire to be able to have complete confidence in the scorers and timers and to know that they will give full cooperation. Certainly, the visitors should not be given any cause for doubt about their work and integrity.

It is always possible to find members of the faculty or citizens in the community who are interested in basketball to act as scorers and timers. It is a mark of good public relations to give these people a contributing role in the sport, and it gives stability to this important aspect of the game if these people continue from year to year. The author had the same timer for all his games for the ten years he was coaching at Springfield College. This man took great pride in his assignment, and he built his calendar, during the season, around the basketball schedule. He was a president of a prominent bank in Springfield, Massachusetts.

PROVISION FOR VISITORS

Adequate accommodations and services should be provided for the press, radio, and television if one is to be assured of the cooperation and support of these agencies. If possible, they should have space where they may work freely and without interference. They should have ready access to all game information. Plans should be made to get statistics to them immediately at the end of each half, and they should have complete information on both teams before the game. If these agencies are to serve and thus help to promote the sport, they must in turn be served.

The visiting team and the officials of the game are guests of the institution. They should be accorded the courtesies to which a guest is entitled. A manager should be assigned to each to look after their needs.

The visiting team should be met upon arrival, the time having been obtained in advance. It should be shown its dressing quarters, given information concerning warm-up and game time, instructed concerning any pre-game ceremonies, provided with towels, advised concerning the disposition of valuables, served in other ways upon request, and made to feel welcome and appreciated by pleasant treatment in every respect.

Likewise, the officials should be greeted upon arrival at the gymnasium and shown to their quarters. They should be provided with towels and protection for their valuables if desired. They should have private dressing room space where they may review rules and discuss the game without interruption. During the progress of the game, they should be accorded all the courtesies to which a guest is entitled. Crowd behavior toward the officials, for which home management is primarily responsible, should be maintained at the level of ladies and gentlemen. In particular, the coach and his team will determine the actions of the crowd very largely by the example which they set.

BASKETBALL STORIES

Stories, if they are good, tend to identify a sport, to set its colorful flavor and history, and to leave an indelible impression on the minds of the listeners. Ford stories are legion and served as the greatest advertising media the Ford automobile has ever enjoyed. Basketball has had a similar experience, and the stories continue to multiply. Many are true; others reflect incidents and trends in the development of the game and identify many of the great leaders. They never fail to delight the public. They are as rich and numerous as those which make up the great tradition of baseball. They run the gamut from the historic exclamation of Dr. Naismith when Dr. F. C. Allen, the first professional coach in the game, asked his advice about accepting an invitation to organize and coach the basketball team at Baker University in Baldwin, Kansas ("You don't coach basketball 'Phog,' you just play it") to the story of the coach who was watching the antics of an inmate of a mental institution through the iron fence surrounding the grounds. The inmate was playing basketball in pantomime. When asked what he was watching, the coach said, "I am scouting that fellow, because if my season becomes any more hectic and disastrous, I shall shortly join him and I want to know how to play him."

Coaches should avail themselves of these stories; they should add to them and use them to promote their sport whenever the opportunity presents itself.

This in part is the role the coach may play in building good public relations for his school through basketball.

4

RECRUITING AND FARM SYSTEMS

Basketball, particularly on the college level, seems to begin with the solicitation of players. Welcome or not, the activity of persuading high school graduates to attend a particular college has become an accepted practice. Coaches spend as much or more time recruiting talent as they do actually coaching their teams.

The competition for athletic talent has become vicious. Little consideration is given to the welfare or best interests of the boy. It does not matter whether the institution offers anything in which the student is interested. The important point is whether he can be persuaded and enticed financially in the hope that he will help to produce a championship team. Such selfish exploitations should be condemned and the ethics of institutions should prohibit rather than silently (sometimes blatantly) condone such practices.

Since it is more or less universally accepted, no one profits in the end. Under existing circumstances, the institution with the most effective recruiting system tends to win; whereas before, the coach with the greatest teaching ability produced the strongest teams.

Concomitant with the work of recruiting goes the practice of buying athletic talent. Institutions and conferences have attempted to dignify this plan by erroneously calling the grants scholarships, when there is seldom any attention whatever given to scholarship. Likewise, conferences, by creating a uniform code by which all institutions shall operate in their bidding, had hopes of eliminating cheating and unfairness which had prevailed previously. It only encouraged institutions to go one step farther. The experiences at North Carolina State, Kentucky, Washington University, U.C.L.A., U.S.C., Indiana, California, and many others furnish the proof. It was also felt that by legislating permission to give board, room, tuition, spending money and whatnot, the sport could still be classed as amateur. How easily we hoodwink ourselves with such a pseudo cloak of respectability! One wonders how those in seats of learning in our country can be so shallow in their thinking. There is even now a proposed "letter of intent" so that a high-pressure scout may bind a prospect and prevent him from freedom of choice thereafter. Essentially, this is a professional contract.

This waste of time and money could be avoided if there were courage and integrity enough to stop this means of recruiting and to permit the students who come voluntarily to an institution to participate on the athletic teams as a matter of their own choice. Of course, this is not likely to happen in the immediate future, but there is certain to be an explosion in time.

Large institutions are now spending more than $100,000 each year, and smaller ones dole out as much as $25,000. Coaching staffs make lists of boys as a season progresses and as the publicity and reports come to their attention. When the tournaments begin, the coaches flock to them and unwittingly and inconsiderately disturb the youngsters and their coaches. After the tournaments, they spend months traveling throughout the country contacting the seniors and their parents. There is not an outstanding athlete anywhere in the country who evades the attention of the aggressive recruiting institutions. The conversation at any gathering of coaches is certain to turn to a discussion of talent from Maine to Southern California. One wonders sometimes how it is possible to have such a thorough record of boys over such a wide expanse of country.

The worst feature of this approach to collegiate athletics is the possible deleterious effect it may have upon the boy who is the pawn in the deal. Boys become confused and upset and are unable to make intelligent decisions. Many become disillusioned, and they get distorted and prejudiced guidance. Often they develop a false sense of values and objectives; they tend to feel that the world owes them a living. Many now send around their own inquiries and accept the highest bid. Then they are reminded of their chattel obligations. These comments, overheard before a contest with one of our "enlightened" universities, are not uncommon: "We are paying you fellows liberally to play. It's about time you began to produce." The language quoted here is a somewhat mild translation of the original.

The foregoing is not an attempt to outline recruiting procedures and practices except by indirection. (Most of the institutions which indulge in the above practices would vehemently deny their validity.) Rather, the purpose is to describe practices which considered, sober judgment would brand as deplorable, with the hope that administrators may not continue to resign themselves to them but that they may be challenged to an administration of athletics on an educational basis comparable to that of other departments of their institutions.

How admirable is the following policy of a prominent institution of higher learning! This policy is conscientiously practiced and produces a student and faculty morale which is the envy of its contemporaries. It is a credit to the wisdom and courage of its administration. Incidentally, its teams have established a commendable record through the years.

ATHLETIC POLICY

IVY COLLEGE

The athletic program at Ivy College is designed, conducted, and administered for the love of the sport, for the general welfare of the player, for the enjoyment of the student body, and for specific training of the young men who attend this college and who expect to enter the coaching and teaching profession. Our chief concern is in producing better citizens to build a stronger nation rather than in producing better athletes to win more games.

This being the athletic philosophy of the college, it follows that we must adhere to certain principles:

(1) No special academic consideration will be afforded any student for athletic ability, nor shall there be any discrimination against an athlete.

(2) Coaches shall meet all the requirements of any and all other faculty members; they shall abide by the same rules and regulations and they shall enjoy the privileges of any and all other faculty members.

(3) The program of athletics shall be as broad as possible with proper emphasis given to the minor sports and the intramural program as well as to the major sports. That program of athletics is best that incorporates the most students.

(4) All players shall be afforded the utmost protection while engaged in competitive sports on the field and while traveling to and from athletic events. Their general health and physical welfare must be the first consideration.

(5) Proper equipment, proper playing conditions, and proper training personnel and medical attention shall be available at all times.

(6) No member of the staff or faculty shall feel that his job depends on wins or losses, although we shall strive to the utmost and give our best to win. Nor shall any job depend on gate receipts, although we shall always endeavor to present a performance worth the price of admission.

(7) Strong, healthy bodies, alert minds, a high sense of sportsmanship, keen enjoyment, and a love of teaching should be the outcomes of the athletic program.

AN EDUCATIONAL PLAN OF RECRUITING AND DEVELOPING MATERIAL

The following presentation is given as an example of a desirable educational plan for recruiting and developing talent. It is in harmony with the policy which has been presented above.

Recruiting as used here means encouraging students who are already members of a student body to try out for teams, and it emphasizes their opportunity to develop into varsity players. It means, further, creating enthusiasm and a wholesome respect for the sports program to the end that they have a desire to play.

In the secondary school the plan would start in the junior high school. In college it would start with the freshman class. All who are interested would be encouraged to try out. No one would be cut off the squad. Boys do a very sound job of self-evaluation, and usually those who find they do not measure up to the more talented withdraw of their own volition in due time.

A thorough program of learning techniques should be introduced, and the speed of reaction of each player should be measured. Personal data on the performance of each should be kept (see Chapter 10). Gradually, the group should be divided into evenly balanced squads of eight and drilled in team tactics. A schedule of intrasquad games should be organized.

Through such a program, those with potential will gradually be recognized. Toward the end of the season, these should be grouped together and several interschool games scheduled for them. These are the potential candidates for the varsity squad in the succeeding year.

During the sophomore and junior years those who do not earn places on the varsity squad should be organized into a junior varsity squad. It is the direct feeder for the varsity for the next year. This squad would have a regular schedule and would play prior to each of the home varsity games. If facilities and staff are available, both a sophomore squad and a junior varsity squad may be organized. A schedule should be arranged for each. All these squads would adopt the pattern of play of the varsity. Their program should be supervised and directed through the varsity coach.

There are many high schools which operate on this basis or one similar to it. In many instances, the varsity squad year after year is made up almost entirely of seniors. They move up to the varsity from the other squads in a normal sequence. Because of their program, they are prepared to fit smoothly into the play of the varsity. They have been trained in the exact system used by the older team.

This plan does not preclude the possibility of players with unusual talent moving directly to the varsity from their junior high, freshman, or sophomore experience. There will be many instances where such procedure will take place. In general, however, the line of succession will be as indicated.

This is truly an educational program and one that emphasizes a primary interest in the development of the individual. Because of this goal, the student is assured of the expenditure of the greatest amount of effort to bring out the best that is in him. This in itself makes the program most inviting, and it provides a valuable activity experience for the many rather than the few. This kind of a program constitutes an honors program in sport.

5

STUDENT MANAGERS

Good student managers are a great asset to the coach, director, and team. The practice of having student managers for athletic teams has a twofold purpose, the most common being to assign the student manager the job of looking after and taking care of equipment. In basketball, for example, he cleans the balls and keeps them inflated to standard pressure, and during practice he watches to see that all equipment is accounted for. These are the types of tasks that are usually assigned to the manager. In most instances this is the extent of his responsibility, so there is little wonder that there is a lack of enthusiasm and competition for the job of manager. Too often the coach must search and beg someone to take the job so that he can be relieved of these duties. It is important and necessary that someone take the responsibility for assignments of this kind; moreover there is value to the individual who assumes the job and conscientiously carries out his assignments, but there are much greater implications.

THE JOB OF THE MANAGER

The wider purpose and by far the more valuable contribution of a student manager is his assumption of the tasks and details of

37

administration incident to the sport. In such a capacity, in addition to performing the menial tasks, the manager becomes representative of both the coach and the director of athletics. When this latter purpose is envisioned as the primary function of the manager, the job offers unlimited educational opportunities. It provides wide participation in and association with a sport for a great number of people. The job becomes an inviting one for which students strive as intently as the players strive for a position on the team. Institutions which have developed a managerial system in this broader sense often find that there are as many aspirants for positions as manager as there are candidates for the team. Where this condition prevails, the sport acquires greater meaning as an integral part of the educational program. It is in this broader sense that the job of student manager is presented in this chapter.

The job will be laid out first and then the plan for carrying it out will be discussed. In general, the job of the manager is to carry out the assignments given to him by the coach, and to assume the responsibility assigned to him by the director of athletics or the person who functions in that capacity. A manager with imagination will look for opportunities to relieve both the coach and the director of as many tasks as possible. There is endless valuable experience that an alert manager can obtain.

The coach has need for someone to see that the facilities are ready for practice. Facilities should be checked fifteen minutes to a half hour before practice. The following are typical points to check: Is the floor clean? Are any lights out? Are the baskets in place and nets in good condition? Are there facilities left by other classes to be removed from the court? Also, the manager should check with the coach before practice to see if any special facilities are needed for that practice, such as a blackboard, bleachers, a classroom, the magnetic board, the rebound ring, conditioning facilities, scoreboard and time clock.

The coach will usually delegate full responsibilities for equipment to the manager. In this connection, the manager should keep the coach advised concerning loss, breakage, deterioration, and the need for additional equipment, supplies, and repairs. Of course, if there is an equipment man, the manager will work closely with him.

DAILY PRACTICE DUTIES

The equipment needs for daily practice include basketballs, which should be kept clean and properly inflated. The schedule for cleaning will depend upon conditions. Some practice facilities are such that balls must be cleaned daily, but others may require cleaning no more than once a week. The manager must determine the schedule. It is important that they be kept clean, because if this is not done regularly, they lose their color, get heavier, and transfer dirt to the hands and soil clothing. The useful life of the balls will be prolonged by proper maintenance. Cleaning and polishing materials for cleaning them and maintaining the leather are on the market. A supply should always be on hand. If basketballs are rubber they may be washed, but leather-covered ones need different care. The manager should learn the art of caring for them. He should know the rule requirement for inflating balls and set up a measuring device for testing them daily. If a ball rack is used, this should be at the court to hold them when not in use.

Practice jerseys are needed when offense works against defense in drills or types of scrimmage. There should be at least two whistles on hand in case a scrimmage is to be conducted. If statistics and records are kept during practice, the charts for recording these data should be on hand.

DUTIES IN PREPARATION FOR GAMES

On days when games are played, the manager has additional duties in handling equipment. He lays out the equipment for each player, checks it out to him and, after the game, checks it back in; or he assists the equipment man in these duties. He calls attention to needs for laundering or cleaning game equipment. He prepares a new ball, which, in some cases, is used for practice the day before a game in order to wear the slickness off it.

In addition to equipment on game days, the manager sees to it that the room used by the team before the game and between halves is ready and that all the materials that the coach uses are at hand: chalk, blackboard, ice bags, oranges, scouting reports, towels—wet and dry—and so forth. He delivers the scorebook to the scorer and checks to see that the timing device and scorer's and timer's signals are on hand. He gets out the foul indicator for the scorer and his identifying coat. He will see that the charts for recording game statistics are at hand.

For games played away from home, after getting the necessary information from the coach, the manager will prepare an itinerary of the trip. A copy will be given to each player the day before departure so that he will have full information. The manager will supervise and check the packing of equipment, provide emergency equipment, see that a first aid bag is packed if a trainer does not accompany the squad, and pack the balls, scorebook, and statistics charts.

DUTIES PERFORMED FOR DIRECTOR OF ATHLETICS

The duties which the manager performs for the director of athletics are those that have to do with finances, player eligibility, records, public relations, and general arrangements for games and trips. In connection with finances, the manager acts for the director on days of games, when preparations are being made for trips with the squad, and when traveling. It is impossible for the director to look after all details, particularly when several teams are competing during a given season. The manager has an opportunity to gain invaluable experience in handling and accounting for funds.

Several days prior to games at home, the manager should

prepare a requisition for all funds needed, so that there will be ample time for preparing vouchers. Funds will be needed for paying guarantees, for officials' fees, and for incidental expenses. This latter includes cost of gum and between-halves refreshment for both the home team and the visitors. If all these items are paid by cash, receipts should be obtained from all who receive funds. If payments are by check, then receipts are not necessary although it is good business to obtain receipts in these instances also. In this way a full accounting can be made for all funds handled by the manager.

For games away from home, the manager should prepare, a week in advance, an estimate for money needed for the trip. This estimate should be presented to the director for approval and the requisition submitted for the funds. The items of expense on a trip may include some or all of the following: transportation, taxi fares, hotel, meals, tips, telephone calls, telegrams, incidental expenses, emergency funds. If definite amounts of expense are known, such as charges for hotel rooms, a check may be requested for these amounts. If large amounts of money are to be handled it is safer to take several checks or travelers' checks than to carry cash. Receipts for all expenditures should be obtained; in this way the manager has a written record of all payments. The amount of the receipts plus the money unspent must equal the total funds requisitioned. In order for a manager to handle this part of his job he must acquaint himself with many aspects of the business management of athletics, with the policies of the director, with schedules, and with the assignment of officials.

All reputable institutions have some kind of eligibility regulations. If the school is a member of a league, that organization has its regulations which govern all members responsible for certifying eligibility.

Most schools keep records of the season's performances. These are filed in the director's office. The manager should see that these records are kept and tabulated at the end of the season for the director. These consist of the scores of games and individual and team playing records, such as free throws, field goals, percentages, fouls committed, total points, and so forth.

The playing record of each individual is used in determining those eligible for awards, so the manager must keep an accurate playing record of each player, tabulate the record at the end of the season, and file it with the director.

THE MANAGER AS HOST

Since the manager is the personal representative of the director at games, the institution is often judged by the manner in which the manager conducts himself as a public relations man. In the first place, for games at home he must act as host to the visiting team. The visitors should be met upon arrival, provided with needed information concerning the game, shown to their dressing room, instructed about the safekeeping of their valuables, provided with towels, shown where the showers and restrooms are located, shown their between-halves and pre-game room, provided with between-halves refreshment, and, in general, made to feel as welcome guests. It is well to provide the visitors with an attendant from arrival to departure so that their needs, inquiries, and problems may be properly handled.

The officials should be met upon their arrival, as well, and shown to their quarters; and their wants and needs should be served in a manner similar to the courtesies offered the visiting team. Both are guests of the school. The officials should have privacy and protection from the public and coaches, and should receive their fees before the contest.

MANAGING THE TRIP

For games which are to be played away, the manager should obtain from the coach all details such as time of departure, number in the party, time of return, and meal schedule; he should then make all arrangements for the director. Advance planning is always more economical and makes for a more pleasant trip, but both the coach and the director should be relieved of this responsibility. These arrangements include:

(a) Transportation. If a school bus is used, it should be requisitioned for a specific time. If private cars are to be used, these should be secured and verification should be made of insurance coverage. If public transportation is to be used, schedules should be investigated, reservations made, and tickets purchased.

(b) Eating. If meals are to be eaten on the trip, arrangements in advance should be made for these. The manager should check with the coach for menus and schedules. Inquiries should be made concerning suitable restaurants and school cafeterias so that the best possible service at the best price may be secured. Reports of previous trips may be used to advantage.

(c) Hotel. If the team is to be away overnight, hotels or motels should be investigated and reservations made well in advance of the trip. Team rates are usually available for both meals and hotel.

(d) Plans for Practice. If a practice is to be held prior to the game, the school should be contacted in advance so that adjustments, if necessary, can be made to accommodate your team.

(e) Additional Transportation. If taxi service is necessary, it is usually possible to get team rates if the total schedule for service can be arranged for at one time.

(f) Squad Meetings. If squad meetings are to be held, the time for these should be obtained from the coach and arrangements made upon registration.

(g) Entertainment and Sight-seeing. If the squad is permitted entertainment or sight-seeing, the schedule for this activity should be planned before the trip.

Handling all these matters in an efficient, prompt, business-like manner is always to the credit of the institution. On extended trips, all of these arrangements can be completed before the trip begins and a complete itinerary handed the players before the trip starts.

The author has had occasion to take his teams on extended trips, several of which have extended over two or three weeks. All of them have been so well organized by efficient managers that they were most pleasant and not strenuous. The players look forward with anticipation to each event on the schedule when trips are well organized. In many cases where the meals have been ordered before the trip began, printed menus have been prepared and placed at each plate.

On one trip a Christmas party was planned enroute and the dining car steward entered into the spirit of the occasion and helped make the party more enjoyable by providing surprises. A theatre party was arranged in New York for the squad by a benefactor of the team because the exact schedule was known in advance. A sight-seeing tour of the nation's capital and visits to historic points and eating places in New Orleans were crowded into the same trip. In addition to all the sight-seeing and fun, seven games were played and won.

On another occasion, a student manager had a meager budget upon which to finance a trip of ten games and three weeks' duration. He worked for a long while making his arrangements and did such an effective job that he was able to show a balance of $4.85 when the trip ended. This is what intelligent, enterprising student management can do. While these examples are of extended trips, it is just as important to plan definitely for short trips, even trips of one day or less. Nothing can be more provoking or upsetting to a team than just prior to or during a trip to have something go wrong because of lack of planning and prior arrangements.

MANAGER'S CHECKLIST

Sufficient material has probably been written to give a comprehensive conception of the magnitude and importance of the job of student manager and of the opportunity for educational experiences for the manager. The details of the job are so diverse and each item so important to the smooth working of a squad that each manager should make a checklist of all items for which he is responsible. These will vary from squad to squad, coach to coach, and school to school. The following check chart, divided into logical groups, will be sufficiently suggestive to alert each manager to the possibilities of his job. The checklist is divided into three divisions: Daily Practice, Home Games, and Trips; these three divisions encompass the details of the total job of the manager.

MANAGER'S CHECKLIST

Daily Practice

court:
a. clean
b. clear
baskets
nets
lights
partitions
ball rack
blackboard
chalk
tipping ring

bleachers
balls:
a. retrieve
b. clean
c. number
scrimmage shirts
whistles
charts
roll
eligibility
spectators
dressing room open

check out practice
clothes:
a. shirt
b. pants
c. socks
d. supporter
e. ankle wrap
f. sweat shirt
laundry
towels
training room
bulletin board

Home Games

check out uni-
forms:
a. shirt
b. pants
c. warmup
d. shoes
e. target socks
f. socks
g. supporter
h. knee pads

chalk
provide host for
visitors
towels for visitors
containers for visi-
tors' valuables
statistics for
visitors
scorebook
timing devices

ice bags
refreshment
towels:
a. wet
b. dry
complimentary
tickets
guarantee check
instructors for pre-
game activity

MANAGER'S CHECKLIST (*Continued*)

between-halves	scorer's jacket	meet officials
room	scorer's and timer's	game instructions
blackboard	horns	for officials
first aid kit	check visitors'	pay officials
stretcher	room:	host for officials
charts for statistics	a. blackboard	key for officials'
needs for press	b. chalk	room
and radio	c. towels	towels for officials
meet opponent	d. refreshment	

Trips

start plans for trip at beginning of season	b. injury pads	pack balls in ball bag
time schedule for travel	c. ankle wrap	issue travel equipment:
time schedule for meals	d. chalk	a. carry-all bags
arrange transportation	e. slate	b. shirt
hotel reservations	f. score book	c. pants
pack extra and special equipment:	g. chart forms	d. warmup
a. change of socks and supporter	arrange for team practice	e. shoes
	prepare complete itinerary for squad	f. socks
	prepare financial estimates	g. target socks
	requisition funds	h. supporter
	receipt book	i. ankle wrap
	prepare absence list	j. practice uniform

MANAGERIAL ORGANIZATION

The job of the manager as described earlier in the chapter and the extensive list of items in the checklist above are characteristic of a managerial setup which requires a large number of managers and a plan of organization which provides definite responsibilities for each. The following plan of organization not only provides the detailed instructions and responsibilities for each manager but it also includes a progressive training program and an automatic plan of selection and succession from one level in the organization to the next.

The Senior Manager

A senior is chosen to be in charge of all managers and the whole program. He is selected from the list of junior managers, and is responsible for organizing the other managers, for delegating their jobs to them, and for supervising their work throughout the season. It is important, as will develop later, that a schedule of duties for the managers should be mapped out at the beginning of the season. The senior manager is directly responsible to the coach and the director of athletics; he reports to them and keeps in touch with them at all times. He should check with his coach daily to learn of any special needs for that day. He accompanies the squad on all trips and takes full charge of looking after their needs on such occasions. He checks to see that all details have been worked out for the trip before departure of the squad from its home base. He tabulates and distributes the team's records, which are filed with him by the sophomore statisticians after each game.

In the normal plan of progression, the senior manager will have worked his way to the top from the position of a trial manager during his freshman year. When the plan is first instituted, the senior manager will be chosen by the coach and director. At the start it will be necessary for them to train and supervise the senior manager rather carefully because he will not be familiar with his many responsibilities. But once the system is functional, a senior manager will ascend to his post fully acquainted with all aspects of his job.

In recognition of his services, the senior manager is eligible to receive a letter award and to be recognized on the same basis as a player who has won his award. Certainly he is not begrudged this honor by the players, because they are aware of the valuable contributions he has made to the sport through his many hours of service in four years.

The Junior Managers

Three juniors are chosen from the sophomore managers to work directly with the senior manager. One of these juniors will become senior manager, so it is important that all understudy their senior most diligently and learn all the facets of his position. At the outset these three juniors will have to be selected. This is usually done by the senior manager with the approval of the coach and director. After the first year under the plan the juniors will be selected from among the sophomore managers.

One junior manager is on duty each day that practice is held and all juniors are present when there is a game at home. A junior, then, is on duty every third practice and at every home game. He is the personal representative of the senior manager. At the direction and under the supervision of the senior manager, he works out the time schedules and work assignments for the other managers and sees that they are posted and delivered to the managers who are under him for the day he is on duty.

On days when games are to be played, one junior manager is assigned to officials, one to the visitors, and one to the home team. Each is fully responsible for all the details incident to his assignments.

In order that each junior manager will have equal practice in preparing for trips in all details, the senior manager will make out a schedule so that each junior receives the same number of trip assignments. This schedule will be planned so that it does not interfere with the daily practice schedule of the junior manager. He will take full charge of all preparations for the trip as indicated on the checklist. If the school travel budget will permit, it is desirable for him to accompany the senior manager on the trip. The experience will be most helpful to him should he later earn the senior position.

At the end of the season, the juniors are eligible to receive a plain sweater award for their services up to that point.

The Sophomore Managers

Six sophomores are chosen from the freshmen who report as managerial candidates before the beginning of the season. For the first year these six sophomores may be selected by the three junior managers and recommended to the senior manager for approval. After the first year the best six freshmen candidates become the sophomore managers for the next season.

The sophomores work under the direction of the juniors. Two sophomores are scheduled to be on duty at each practice. This means that they are on duty every third practice. At least one must be present on the floor at all times in case he is needed by the coach for some special detail. If scrimmages are held, the sophomores may act as officials if the coach requests them for this purpose. The sophomores are in direct charge of the freshman candidates who are assigned to duty on the same day. All of the work of the sophomores is done at the court or in the equipment room. They, with the freshmen, are workhorses of the managerial system, the laborers who hope to be worthy of their toil. They are striving to impress their junior managers so that they may be the successful candidates to move on to the more executive jobs as junior managers.

On home-game days the sophomores are all on duty to help whenever needed. The sophomores always keep the game statistics and tabulate the data for distribution to the press, the visitors, and the home team and to the senior manager at the end of the first half and at the end of the game.

The Freshman Candidates

Before the season begins, invitations are issued through the school paper, the school public address system, at assemblies, and on the bulletin boards for applicants for basketball managers. A date is set for a meeting at which interested freshmen, together with the sophomores, junior, and senior managers, assemble. The senior manager presides and explains the details of the managerial system. He introduces his staff and invites those who desire to try out to sign up. There should be no limit on the number of applicants. In large schools as many as fifty have signed for duty. A short time later another meeting is called for further discussion and instructions. At this meeting a schedule of assignments is passed out to trial managers and managers. A copy is also posted on the basketball bulletin board. Provision is made at this time for making changes in assignments should this become necessary during the season. Also, arrangements are made for future meetings if these become necessary.

The candidates are divided into equal groups and assigned to practices so that a trial manager is not on duty oftener than every other practice day. The freshmen work at the direction of the sophomores. They do all the menial tasks incident to managing. The spirit with which they accept these jobs is one good criterion as to their suitability for advancement. They are usually not assigned on game days but may be used if needed.

AN ORGANIZATION CHART

This organization plan with the number of managers indicated is considered ideal. The demands on the time of anyone are not excessive, there is sufficient competition to keep everyone on his toes, and the goals are sufficiently rewarding to create desire and incentive to become a manager.

This plan as described here provides for managers for just one squad. Most schools have two or more squads competing, but the plan is adaptable to more than one. If all squads are practicing at the same time and are on the same floor, no change in assignments is necessary. If, however, the squads practice at different hours, then either the rotation of boys on duty will have to be more frequent or the time on duty each practice day will have to be longer. The juniors would always be assigned to take turns in traveling with the other squads. For games at home, the sophomores take over the duties of the juniors and the trial managers take over the duties of the sophomores.

This plan is worked out on the basis of four classes. In the senior high school where there are only three classes, six junior managers should be chosen. They would assume the duties of both the sophomores and the juniors in the original plan, part always on hand for the court work normally assigned to the sophomores and the others assuming the assignments of juniors. There should, of course, be a rotation of the assignments. The sophomores would be on trial, and as many as report should be permitted to sign up.

An organization chart showing the plan for the managerial system described is shown so that one may better visualize the plan.

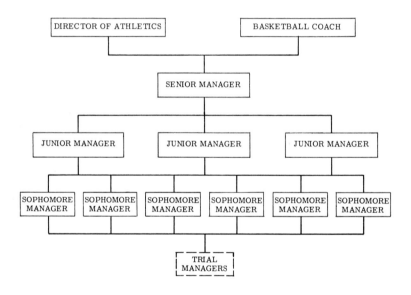

PLAN OF SELECTION

Mention has been made repeatedly concerning the selection of freshman candidates to become sophomore managers, sophomores to become juniors and a junior to become a senior manager. The process of selection should be made as impersonal as possible. A rating scale has been worked out as a means of determining those with the best qualifications and to give partial objectivity to the process of selection. Managers are required to rate the assistants under them each week, and the ratings are turned into the coach. Thus, as many as twenty separate ratings and no fewer than eight by each rater will be available on each manager. With this accumulation a fairly valid and reliable evaluation can be secured.

Each sophomore manager rates each freshman who serves under him during the week. Each junior manager rates each sophomore who serves under him during the week. The senior manager rates each junior manager each week. At the end of the season, the ratings for each candidate are tabulated. The candidates are rated in order on the basis of the accumulated ratings. As a further check the junior managers are asked to look over the ratings of the beginners and to make independent comments on the basis of their own observation of any of them. The senior manager is asked to study, similarly, the ratings which the juniors have made of the sophomores. In addition to the ratings which the senior manager has filed on the juniors, the coach and the director of athletics file their vote for the junior of their choice. The ratings of the senior manager constitute his vote. Thus three votes are cast for senior manager. If there is no agreement, a conference is held to discuss and make the final selection. The coach or director may at any time during the season record observations which he may choose to make on any manager at any level. These observations shall be considered with the managers' ratings.

A RATING SCALE

The rating scale shown below contains six items and provides for a five-point scale. A numerical value from one to five is given to each point on the scale. These numerical values are added to get an accumulative score for each item and the total scores for the total scale are added. The latter score is used to determine the order of rating of the candidates. Extremely low scores in any one item may be studied before the final decision is made. Indications of progress or retrogression should be considered also. A sample of this rating scale is shown below.

MANAGERS' WEEKLY RATING SCALE

NAME: _____ DATE: _____

PUNCTUALITY	Seldom on time or ready	Late occasionally	Usually on time or ready	Always on time or ready	Always ahead of time
INITIATIVE AND LEADERSHIP	No initiative	Follows	Leads occasionally	Usually leads	Shows marked leadership
DEPENDABILITY	Irresponsible	Somewhat lax	Occasionally fails to do job	Usually completes job	Carries out assignments without fail
ATTITUDE	Antagonistic	Negative	Passive	Cooperative	Enthusiastic
RELATION WITH OTHERS	Rude	Thoughtless	Agreeable	Shows consideration for others	Very diplomatic
JUDGEMENT	Erratic	Immature	Consistent	Usually makes right move	Always makes correct decisions

(Check one item in each row and file at the end of each week.)

6

RULES AND OFFICIATING

Coaches should be intimately acquainted with the mechanics of officiating and they should be thoroughly conversant with the rules and the official interpretation of them. They are primarily responsible for the administration of the game which they coach, and they cannot possibly assume this responsibility in an intelligent manner unless they become expert in their knowledge of the rules and of their administration.

Coaches have been remiss in this aspect of their jobs and their obligation to the institutions they represent. The common refrain that they are "too occupied with the immediate job of turning out a winning team" is hardly defensible. How can one evaluate justly the work of an official if he does not know what the official is supposed to do in a given situation? How can one coach his team intelligently within the rules if he does not have a thorough understanding of them and know their intent?

THE DEVELOPMENT OF OFFICIALS' ASSOCIATIONS

Officials are to be commended for their efforts to upgrade their work. During the early 1920's officials began to meet in local and area groups to study the rules and to discuss more effective methods of officiating. Before this period, officiating was largely a personal matter. It was often a question of finding or persuading someone to work games. It was common practice for schools to send their entire schedules to an official who was found to be satisfactory and ask him to work as many games as he could and then supply someone for the remainder.

Out of these beginnings, local, regional and state organizations began to form. Finally, a National Association of Approved Basketball Officials came into being. The efforts of John Brown, the first executive secretary of the organization, were largely responsible for its creation. Its objective was to strive for uniform interpretation and administration of the rules throughout the country, to develop a standard set of methods and procedures for officiating, to provide a program for training and certifying new officials in order to provide an adequate supply of competent arbiters, and to contribute to rules legislation from the experience and point of view of the official.

The national organization finally became international in scope and adopted the title of International Association of Approved Basketball Officials. This association now boasts over 10,000 members organized under more than 160 boards in 28 states (including Hawaii), the District of Columbia, the United States Armed Services and five foreign countries.

This organization grew and developed independent of high schools, colleges, and clubs because these groups did little or nothing to provide for their own needs. It is not surprising, therefore, that as the officials' organization grew in strength and importance, it began to make demands upon the institutions which it served. In some instances open clashes over fees and other regulations arose. The lack of a close cooperative relationship between the officials' organization and institutions was the primary cause of most problems.

Although it is recognized that officials are motivated by their fees, and understandably so, it is also true that, through their organizations, they have made valuable contributions toward upgrading the caliber of officiating.

THE ROLE OF INSTITUTIONS IN OFFICIATING

Institutions, conferences, state organizations and the National Federation of State High School Athletic Associations began to recognize the fact that those who create the necessity for officials must also determine and approve the plan under which they shall function. They must set the standards. As a result the State High School Associations have undertaken the huge task of organizing officials' groups to supply their needs. High schools in every state have a greater demand for officials than any other group. They now have approximately 35,000 registered officials. In many states where the International Association of Approved Basketball Officials has membership, the two groups work co-operatively. The commissioners of college conferences have assumed the responsibility for the officials in their conferences. Meetings for the discussion of rules are held by state associations, leagues, conferences, and officials' organizations throughout the United States. Officials' groups continue to meet periodically throughout the basketball season. A national interpreter has been appointed to travel about the country to conduct meetings so that the same story will be told to each group.

In September each year the I.A.A.B.O. meets in New York for a meeting on rules and the mechanics of officiating. A transcript of this meeting, which is conducted by the national interpreter, is distributed to every district board in the United States and foreign countries.

The National Association of College Commissioners meets annually for an interpretation and demonstration meeting, which is conducted by the national interpreter. A transcription of this meeting is distributed to all the member colleges in this association. Each conference in this association has a follow-up meeting.

A "Case Book" which contains several hundred official interpretations is published each year and thousands of copies are distributed. The national interpreter releases official interpretations each month and answers questions throughout the year on play situations that arise during the season.

The National Federation of State High School Athletic Associations publishes a booklet on the mechanics of officiating. This is brought up-to-date each year, and is available to anyone interested. The National Association of College Commissioners publishes its officiating manual and distributes it to all its registered officials. The I.A.A.B.O. publishes an officiating manual, which is distributed to its members. This organization also distributes materials to enlighten the spectator so that he may gain a better appreciation of the game. This is good public relations.

THE ROLE OF THE COACH

These developments have made tremendous improvement in the administration and enjoyment of the game. But even with the present progress, the coaches have not yet come into the picture to the extent that they must in order that a mutual relationship between the coach and the official can be developed. The coaches must be as familiar with the rules as the official. In every comparative test that the author has made, the coaches (who are not also officials) have rated at least 15 per cent below the officials in their knowledge of the rules. (The comparison is even more disparaging when the mechanics of officiating are involved.) It was most startling to learn that the rule on charging, which was changed in 1954, was known by very few coaches in 1958. And, yet, these same coaches are often violent in the criticism of officials who are doing an excellent job, in most cases, in administering the rules. The coaches have as great a responsibility in attending rules meetings as do the officials, but they seldom meet this obligation.

A WORKABLE PLAN

A most effective and satisfactory plan for mutual relationship between coaches and officials was developed in the Pacific Coast Conference some years ago. Twice each year the coaches and the officials who were chosen for conference games met for the purpose of rules interpretations and discussion of common problems in the administration of their games. Such things as the conduct of coaches, coaches' talking to officials, tactics of players and teams that implied attempts to influence officials, the mechanics of some officials, interpretations and demonstrations of rules and play situations were discussed freely and frankly. These discussions resulted in the adoption of very definite standards, but, best of all, they produced an understanding and friendliness which were not previously possible. It also was very apparent that a greater trust and confidence had developed. These meetings were always held in the fall before competition began and in the spring after competition was finished so that emotional factors were eliminated.

The results of this procedure became widely known and similar plans were adopted by other groups. This plan is actually the forerunner of the present plan for supervision of officials through the office of conference commissioners. High school leagues could profit immeasurably by such a plan and its continued cultivation. Our amateur game should always strive for cordial, mutual relationships between coaches and officials.

AN INSTITUTIONAL PROGRAM

A definite program is needed at each institution to bring about the type of relationship that will help to build an atmosphere at games which is conducive to good sportsmanship. Such a program is outlined in the following comments:

1. The coach must set the example for his team and for his followers. He is the leader, and he must set the example for

onlookers. The conduct of the coach can incite or calm his players and the spectators. If he loses his temper and reacts unreasonably toward the officials, the crowd will more than likely do the same. If, however, he accepts the decisions of the officials and asks his players and the spectators to do likewise, there will be no difficulty. A coach should remember that if he spends much of his time concentrating on the officials he is neglecting his team and will be unable to give it needed advice at the proper time.

2. The officials are guests of the institution which they are serving. They are entitled to the courtesies commonly accorded a guest.

3. The public address should be utilized at the beginning of the season to acquaint the spectators with rules changes and interpretations. During the progress of a game, explanations of questionable situations may be given. This tends to clear up misunderstandings. An informed public is usually a cooperative public.

4. Helpful information may be included in the program.

5. Informative broadcasts over radio and television are useful.

6. The local paper is a valuable instrument for promoting a better understanding of the game.

Because the basketball rules are comparatively simple and few in number and because the spectators are so close to the play, they feel that they know the rules and can officiate better than those engaged for the purpose. Unfortunately, the spectator does not know the basic principles which the official uses for a guide in making his decisions. If these guides are given to the spectators, they will be more understanding.

INTERSQUAD SCRIMMAGES

There is great value to the coach, to his players, and to officials in having intersquad scrimmages officiated. Officials need practice in officiating before the regular playing season begins, the players need the experience of playing under regular officiating conditions, and the coach needs to be freed from the responsibility of officiating so that he may concentrate on the action of his team.

Officials welcome the opportunity to officiate intersquad or interschool scrimmages. The author has made it a practice to invite officials to work out at a number of his scrimmages each year, and the officials always respond with enthusiasm. The players welcome the experience of practicing under game conditions, and they are able to adjust their habits of play to a strict administration of the rules and thus avoid many mistakes when the regular playing season begins. It is strongly recommended that every coach have several of his scrimmages officiated by trained officials during the pre-season preparation.

RULES DRILLS FOR PLAYERS

The players should be thoroughly conversant with the essential playing rules. A thorough understanding of the rules begets greater conformity to the rules in playing habits; and a knowledge of the rules begets a better understanding and acceptance of the decisions of the officials and in turn fewer emotional disturbances because of the officiating during the progress of the game.

It is soon apparent to officials when players have a thorough knowledge of the rules. This knowledge keeps officials more alert and it often prevents them from making inadvertent mistakes.

At the beginning of the season it is desirable to explain the changes in the rules and to demonstrate the effect these changes will have on the playing habits of the players. As plays and tactics are presented and demonstrated to the squad, it is helpful to the players if the freedom and limitations provided in the rules are also explained.

Rules drills in play situations during the season, at lecture periods, and particularly on trips, are both stimulating and educational. In order to motivate rules study, the author has offered prizes for questions on rules he could not answer. It is surprising how many times one can be trapped by catch questions. The questioner is always required to state the rule when an error is made.

Rule books and case books should always be available for the use of the squad. The official examination is often given to the squad so that they may test their record against the requirements for approved officials. This is one way to develop a respect for them because the players never do as well on these tests as do the officials.

7

EQUIPMENT

Equipment for basketball consists primarily of wearing apparel for the players for practice, for playing, for pre-game and side line wear, balls, ball containers, and baggage for carrying equipment on trips. These needs are relatively simple and inexpensive, a fortunate situation in view of the constant concern over financing athletic programs. Few sports can be administered with less expense. One can, of course, be elaborate and extravagant; but this is not necessary. A team can be neat in its appearance and not be expensively attired. The equipment budgets for high schools as surveyed by Forsythe [1] average approximately $100.00 for schools under 500; approximately $150.00 for schools with enrollments from 500 to 1500; and $265.00 for schools with enrollments over 1500. A college budget will range from $500.00 to $2500.00.

Every coach is faced with the problem of equipment. He wants his team to look well on the court. After all, there is fashion in sports. If there is a spark of the actor in the coach (and what coach does not have some "ham" about him?), he strives for something unique and individual in the appearance of his squad. Some are more artistic than others at gaining at-

---

[1] Charles E. Forsythe, *Administration of High School Athletics,* 3rd ed., (Englewood Cliffs, N.J., Prentice-Hall, Inc., 1954), p. 264.

tractive and pleasing effects. Many, however, merely follow the trends of the times and accept whatever some salesman persuades them to buy.

GUIDES FOR PURCHASING EQUIPMENT

There are standards or criteria which can be helpful guides to all coaches in the purchase of equipment. Among these are appearance, cost, durability, utility and comfort. The first three are discussed specifically in the following paragraphs. Utility and comfort are factors throughout the discussion of equipment.

Appearance has many features. First of all, the tailoring of a garment is very important. Some of our equipment suppliers have the knack of being able to make a silk purse out of a sow's ear. Others can take the same quality material and produce a garment which when worn creates a sloppy-looking person. As one is selecting equipment, he should have someone model samples for him so that the tailoring may be observed. It costs no more for expert tailoring. Therefore, one should deal only with those firms which provide the best.

School colors are used to make up uniforms. Various combinations of these colors are used to produce unique and distinctive effects. Tastes vary in this respect. It should be borne in mind, however, that too much gingerbread more often than not produces a gaudy appearance. It is better, therefore, to curb the desire to be too flamboyant with the arrangement of colors if artistic rather than bizarre effects are desired.

There is one characteristic of appearance that must always be kept in mind. It is distinctiveness or contrast with the uniform of the opponent. This is for practical purposes. Basketball is played at a rapid pace, and it is necessary for players to be able to identify teammates and distinguish opponents instantly. Therefore, equipment designed so that it affords instant recognition without being extreme is desirable. There is reason in this connection for bright colors, for target socks with stripes rather than plain colors, and for colored shoes. Plain colors are not as quickly identified as vivid colors, stripes, or checks.

Cleanliness and tidiness are characteristics of appearance. Regardless of the type of uniform, if it is soiled and wrinkled it loses its attractiveness. There is no excuse for dirty, soiled uniforms. Laundry and cleaning should be used as needed to keep equipment clean. They are actually economical, in prolonging the life of equipment. Wrinkling can be controlled in two ways. If equipment is kept on hangers, it will not wrinkle as readily as when it is folded or stuffed in traveling bags. Flannels and woolen warm-up garments do not wrinkle easily. When hung up after unpacking, wrinkles disappear. These materials are much preferred to nylon, satin, and the like which look as if they have been slept in after the first wearing or packing. The shiny appearance is offset by the untidy condition.

Cost must always and should always be considered when purchasing equipment. Because of public relations policies, politics, special privilege, favoritism, and budget practices, it is not always possible to capitalize on the most advantageous buying opportunities. It often becomes necessary or expedient to purchase locally and without the usual discounts afforded educational institutions. Institutional prices are from 25 to 30 per cent below retail prices. By astute shopping, it is possible to save another 25 or 30 per cent for top quality merchandise. Many institutions, particularly public schools in large cities and state institutions, require bids. When this practice is followed, it is essential that the quality of the merchandise be exactly and carefully specified. Unless this practice is followed, it is not possible to evaluate and compare bids.

Examples of specifications may be helpful to the reader. There are many grades and types of basketballs. One should, therefore, describe exactly the type and grade desired. A particular ball made by a certain manufacturer may be specified by giving the identifying number such as "the Wilson Jet ball No. 1000. Then, since the item is to be open to bids, the phrase, "or equal," should be added. Such a description definitely defines the type of construction (a molded ball of specified quality), the type of cover (leather of a specific grade and color), and the width and depth of seams. A cross-sectional sample to show construction may be required for comparison purposes if experience in- dicates that purchasing agents are not capable of making intelligent comparisons. The same procedure may be followed in the case of shoes.

Durability. There is no economy in purchasing inferior quality equipment. It neither wears long nor looks well. By the same token, the purchase of luxury items cannot be justified. The criteria should be durability and, as previously discussed, appearance. For example, nylon and twill are very durable wearing apparel, and this justifies the extra cost.

CARE OF EQUIPMENT

Suits and warmup garments should be cleaned regularly. The acid from perspiration, if left in these garments, will shorten the life of them substantially. If the uniforms are made of material which does not shrink and will not fade from washing, then they should be washed and not dry cleaned. This process is cheaper and in addition cleans the garments more thoroughly.

When the season is over all uniforms should be thoroughly cleaned before storing. If the materials may be damaged by moths, then repellents should be put in them for protection.

If equipment is in need of repair or reconditioning, this should be done before it is stored. The best time to inspect equipment and to make judgments on whether to discard, recondition, or purchase new items is at the close of the season. Most schools do not have facilities for repairing and reconditioning equipment, but there are firms which specialize in these services. They do excellent work in restoring equipment so that it is usable for one or more additional seasons. It is profitable to consult these organizations concerning repair problems. Usually they operate locally but some are national or at least sectional in scope. Their

representatives are always glad to call to discuss and evaluate
reconditioning jobs.

S H O E S

The importance of comfortable, perfect fitting shoes that grip
the floor firmly cannot be overstressed.

Weight and wearing qualities are other features which should
be considered when selecting shoes. There is no article of wearing
apparel more important to a player. It is of such great importance
that the coach should supervise the fitting of shoes personally.

There are two criteria to guide the coach. First, he should be
sure that the big toe is at least one-half inch from the end of the
shoe. This permits the foot to move within the shoe when a
player is making a sudden stop without causing the toe to rub
against the end of the shoe. Unless this much freedom is provided, sore toes and blisters are very likely to develop.

Second, the shoe should be wide enough so that the foot, when
one's weight is placed over it, will not spread over the edge of the
soles. A shoe that fits too tightly is more likely to permit blisters
to develop. Players, if permitted to select their own shoes, will
almost invariably choose a shoe which is at least a half size too
small. The danger of blisters is greater with tightly fitting shoes
because of the greater amount of friction induced between the
foot and the shoe. A player with blistered feet is lost to a team
for two weeks, long enough to deprive him of his chances of
making a place on the squad.

As an aid in the protection of the feet, two pairs of socks
should be worn. Two pairs of socks help to cushion the terrific
pounding which the feet are required to take. In addition they
tend to reduce the effect of rubbing between the shoes and the
feet. Of course, two pairs of socks should be worn when the
shoes are being fitted.

All shoes do not grip the floor equally. The quality of gripping
is a measure of the coefficient of friction between the sole of the
shoe and the floor. Gripping ability is dependent upon the weight

with which the shoe presses directly against the floor, the finish of the floor, and the characteristics of the sole of the shoe. A soft rubber soled shoe will grip more firmly than a hard rubber sole, but the soft sole will not wear as long as the hard soled shoe.

One may test the relative gripping ability of shoes by the simple method of putting a weight in the shoes and then measuring the amount of force exerted in a horizontal direction, which is necessary to start the shoe to slip. The greater force indicates a better gripping quality.

The practice of using rosin on the soles of the shoes has doubtful value. If it has any value it is short lived. Rosin, if it is sticky, will pick up dirt from the floor which in turn will reduce the gripping effect of the shoe. A sounder practice is to keep both the floor and the sole of the shoes free from dirt for better gripping.

The use of leather-top shoes for basketball has practically ceased. Field testing of leather-topped shoes demonstrated the fact that the soles wore out much faster than the uppers. Unless soles could be replaced, it was not profitable to pay the extra cost for the leather uppers. Shoes which are constructed so that the life of the sole and the upper is about equal represent the best balance. Those shoes which wear the longest represent the best investment if the other qualities are comparable.

The oxford type of basketball shoe is preferred by some players. The question is often raised about the lack of ankle support when this style of shoe is worn. It is doubtful if much valuable support is gained from the high top shoe. Certainly more flexibility of the ankle joint is gained by the oxford-type shoe. It is very doubtful, however, if any great advantage is gained by either style of shoe. The choice is largely one of personal preference.

The only known difference between the two types of shoes is the tendency for the low-cut shoe to slip off the foot. In some cases, a player has deliberately pulled the shoe off his foot in order to get an uncharged time out. This, of course, is unethical practice. If such practice persists or increases it may be necessary to take drastic rules action to stop it.

PROTECTION OF FEET AND ANKLES

It is not the purpose of this chapter to discuss the care and prevention of injuries. However, the feet and ankles are such an important part of a basketball player and any athlete, that comments on the use of tape for the feet and ankle wraps are included here.

The unusual amount of starting and stopping in basketball causes even the properly protected foot to develop calluses on the heel, the side and bottom of the feet, and the toes. If these calluses are permitted to increase, eventually a deep blister will develop. Therefore, prevention is a desirable procedure. The use of adhesive tape is the simplest form of prevention. As the callous begins to form, two layers of adhesive tape should be placed over the affected area. This tape should be worn continuously until the hard skin softens and can be sloughed off by rubbing. Usually a week is enough time to soften the skin sufficiently so that the excess can be removed. Then, the use of the tape should cease until the callus begins to form again.

The greatest danger of injury in basketball is that of receiving a sprained ankle. This is because one stops so abruptly and jumps so often that there is the possibility of alighting and throwing the weight of the body on the side of the foot so that the external lateral ligaments are unduly stretched. As a consequence, added support to guard against injury from these extreme pressures is desirable.

The author has always required all his basketball candidates to wear ankle wraps for all practices. If a candidate has a history of sprained ankles, then he is required to tape his ankles. As a result of this precaution no serious problems with sprained ankles have ever been encountered. Tape for calluses and ankle wraps for prevention of sprains are standard basketball equipment.

8

CONDITIONING

The improvement in performance during the past 20 years has been as phenomenal as at any stage in athletic history. Improvement in facilities, equipment, and coaching procedures, and the application of scientific principles in the analysis of playing techniques have all contributed to this great advance. The most recent element in the game to receive attention is that of training and conditioning. Too many of the theories and practices of the past have been based upon unsound principles or no principles at all. As a consequence, much precious time and effort has been wasted and in many cases adverse results have been created. The work of Westering[1] has proved this point beyond a shadow of a doubt. He gave two parallel groups conventional and scientific procedures; and those taking the scientific procedures excelled the others in every respect and attained their superior condition in half the time.

The principles involved in conditioning have been available for years but they have not been applied. No doubt the desire to excel and the intense competition of recent years have directed coaches to explore every possible aspect of the literature with the

---

[1] Forrest Westering, "A Comparison of Two Types of Physical Conditioning Programs on High School Athletes" (Master's thesis, Colorado State College, 1960).

hope of finding something that could be exploited in the interest of winning. Karpovich [2] has brought together the pertinent physiological research on conditioning and has shown its practical application to sports.

Physical conditioning for basketball is the procedure by which one builds sufficient body strength and endurance to permit him to play at a maximum level throughout a game. He must be prepared not only to meet the requirements of play of his own team but the demands forced upon him by reason of the pace set by his opponents.

The greatest demand for strength is in jumping. The requirement in this aspect of basketball is particularly great when a short player is pitted against one who is much taller. The shorter player may be able to cope with his taller opponent early in the game but if he has not built up a reserve of strength to carry him through the entire game with the extra effort necessary to overcome his height handicap, the taller player will dominate the play toward the end. This is the time when condition is put to its severest test.

BUILDING STRENGTH

The source of strength is muscle. The strength of a muscle is directly proportional to its cross sectional area, varying from 90 to 140 pounds per square inch. Research has determined that, having mastered the technique in jumping, one's improvement thereafter is directly proportional to the increase in leg strength. If, therefore, one desires to add to his height by increasing his ability to jump vertically, he must increase his leg strength. Simply, this means he must build leg muscles. The importance of adding distance to one's vertical jumping is realized when one considers that being able to reach higher by the length of the joint of a finger is sufficient to control the basketball.

There are two principles that control the growth of muscles beyond that which takes place through the exercise producing normal growth and development. Growth takes place only through exercise, but building muscle quickly for athletic purposes requires that one exercise for short periods with the muscle under extreme stretch. Thus, the principles of overloading the muscle and exercising for short, intermittent intervals have been developed. These two principles need to be thoroughly explained so that they may be practically applied by coaches.

A muscle is overloaded for the purpose of increasing its cross section and thus its strength. This is accomplished by progressively increasing the amount of work required—for instance, by adding to the weight which is lifted at each exercise period or by increasing the force which a muscle is required to resist. The initial load for starting the exercise should be equal to the weight or force that the muscle is able to lift or exert before the conditioning exercises are begun. Since in basketball primary interest is in building leg strength in order to increase the ability to jump, leg lift strength may be used to determine the initial load. The common procedure is to measure the strength of the plantar flexors of each leg by means of a tensiometer. If a tensiometer is not available, a crude measure may be determined by means of a spring balance. The procedure is as follows: the subject sits on a table with his foot at right angles to the leg. A strap is placed around the foot at the transverse arch. The spring balance is hooked to the strap so that a pull may be exerted in a direction parallel to the leg and away from the head of the subject. The subject resists the pull. The force of the pull should be increased until the subject is unable to resist further. The amount of the force at failure is recorded. The sum of the force for each leg is used as the initial weight for the beginning of the conditioning exercises. Figure 1, p. 72, illustrates the procedure.

If facilities and instruments are not available for determining the initial load, estimates may be made. For the protection of the individual it will be safer to begin with a lighter load. If

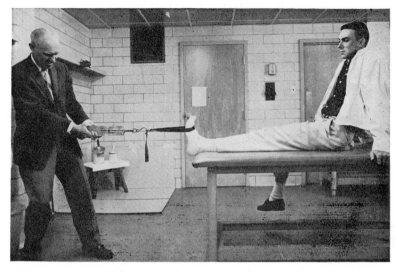

Figure 1. *A practical method of measuring plantar flexor strength by use of spring scale.*

too light a load is chosen at the outset, the technique for increasing the load at subsequent exercise periods will automatically correct the error. One-half the body weight is a safe load with which to begin.

Several exercise programs have been studied. From the standpoint of simplicity of administration and results obtained, the heel raising exercise is recommended. This exercise produces results comparable to a combined program of deep knee bends and toe raising. It is much simpler to administer and is easier to control and thus far safer for the subjects.

Heel raising consists of placing the ball of the foot across the rounded or padded edge of a two-inch board which has been securely anchored and rising as high as possible on the toes with the initial weight as determined above carried across the shoulders. The exercise is conducted in three stages. The first stage consists of rising ten times in continuous movement, then resting for one minute. The second stage is a repetition of the first. The third stage continues until the subject is unable to raise the weight. When the muscles of the legs begin to tremble or the calf muscles feel very warm, the exercise should be discontinued even though the subject might be able to continue.

The load for each succeeding exercise period is determined by adding five pounds to the load for the previous period plus one pound for each lift in excess of ten during the third stage. This procedure is an arbitrary one but does assure a progressive increase in the load and continued muscle growth. If one selects a load below the strength of the individual for the initial exercise period, the subject will be able to raise an excessive number of times during the third stage. This fact automatically adjusts the load to the strength of the subject for the next exercise period.

The exercises should be administered every other day. Kruse [3] found that exercises conducted under the extreme condition of overloading retarded growth if repeated more often than every other day. Three times per week produced better results than two or four times per week, or daily exercises. Muscle under extreme stress fatigues quickly and recovers slowly. Apparently full recovery is not effected within twenty-four hours. This accounts for the necessity of the principle of *intermittency* in conducting exercises to build strength.

RESULTS OF PROGRAM

How long should conditioning exercises be continued? Naturally, there is a limit for each individual. Tests have been extended for as long as twelve weeks with continued improvement. They have been conducted throughout a season with benefit. The answer depends somewhat upon the standards desired. It has been found that a program extending over four or five weeks produces a state of physical condition which will meet all the demands of the most extreme conditions in the present-day game. Jumping ability has been increased as much as eight inches. In

---

[3] Robert Kruse, "Effects of Isometric and Isotonic Exercises on Elbow Flex or Muscle Groups" (Doctoral dissertation, Springfield College, 1956).

no case has anyone failed to improve as much as one inch. Leg strength has been increased as much as 160 pounds!

The weight training exercises present some problems. In the first place, it is more or less an individual activity and, therefore, is time consuming. As a consequence, if the program can be set up and conducted before the date on which practice begins, it is a distinct advantage. It is most desirable to use bar bells for the training program, but these are expensive so may be prohibitive in many schools. Sandbags, buckets of sand, or improvised bar bells may be devised. Padding is recommended for the bars so that the weight on the shoulders of the subject is not injurious.

SAFETY MEASURES

There is some element of danger in weight training. As the weight is increased (it may exceed 400 pounds) there is danger that the subject may lose his balance during exercise or injure himself when putting the weight down or raising it to his shoulders. As a consequence, the weights should be hung from the ceiling and a block and tackle arrangement devised so that the weights may be lowered or lifted to and from the shoulders at the beginning and end of exercise. This technique prevents the weights from dropping and avoids the necessity of the subject's lifting the weights to his shoulders with the possibility of back injury.

An ideal safety arrangement is to set up some vertical standards spread apart the width of the weights on the bar. These standards are double on each side, and should be anchored to the floor and ceiling. Pin holes are drilled through the standards at six-inch intervals to accommodate different height players. Steel pins are inserted in the holes at the proper height. These pins hold up the bar so that a player need only bend his legs slightly to get his shoulders under the bar. The back can be kept vertical for protection; and if the player should lose his balance while exercising, the pins will catch the bar so that accidents are

Figure 2. *Starting position for heel*   Figure 3. *Extended position in heel*
          lift exercise.   *lift exercise.*

avoided. This type of safety apparatus is shown in Figures 2
and 3.

If the above devices are not available, the subject should be
assisted by teammates. The weights should be lifted and placed
on the subject's shoulders at the beginning. At the end, teammates should remove the weights. During exercise, teammates
should stand by to support the weights in case the subject should
lose his balance.

BUILDING ENDURANCE

Exercises to produce endurance are somewhat different in
character from those used to develop strength. The overload
principle is not a factor. Endurance is measured by the ability
of the circulatory system to remove the waste products of
exertion from the muscles and to deliver food to them. The
level of endurance is indicated by the degree to which the per-

son is able to perform at a high, constant rate without the onset of fatigue.

In order to build up endurance, the body must increase its capillary system about the muscle fibers so that the exchange of waste products for food may take place more rapidly. This is brought about by exercises performed at an intense rate. In other words, to build endurance quickly, repetition at a rapid rate is necessary.

While there is no limit to exercises that one might use, three drills have been used effectively in building endurance: The Carlson Spot Run technique,[4] sit-ups, and push-ups. The Carlson Spot Run consists of running in place for ten seconds with a ten-second rest. This is repeated ten times. The feet are raised just high enough to clear the floor. The cadence is as rapid as the subject can move. When a standard of eighty steps per ten seconds can be maintained for the duration of the ten repetitions, the subject has sufficient endurance to meet the severest demands of a basketball game. If greater endurance is desired, the standard can be raised, more repetitions can be added, or the time may be increased.

Sit-ups are performed in the usual manner with the hands clasped behind the head. The legs are kept horizontal and the feet are held by a teammate. On each sit-up the elbow touches the knee, that is, the right elbow touches the left knee and on the next sit-up, the left elbow touches the right knee. Since the players work in pairs, when one finishes they exchange positions so that the other may take his sit-ups. This exercise is carried on for two minutes at as rapid a pace as possible. A standard of ninety sit-ups should be attained by each player. When this exercise is conducted intensely, some players incur abrasions on the back from the friction between the body and the floor. To avoid this condition, it is wise to lie on one's sweat clothes.

The third exercise, the push-ups, are performed on the fingertips for a period of thirty seconds. The chin must touch on each

---

[4] H. C. Carlson, "Basketball Research in Fatigue," National Association of Basketball Coaches, 1956.

push-up. A standard of twenty-five push-ups in thirty seconds is the goal. A few players exceed this standard.

These exercises can be taken in a group. Since they are all done by time, the coach or someone can be assigned to act as timekeeper. A whistle can be blown to start and stop each inning in the spot run and the sit-ups and push-ups, with each player counting his own performance. In order for each player to study his development, a record may be kept of his performance. A convenient card for keeping records is shown in the accompanying figure. The cards are distributed before the exercises are given, and the records will serve as motivators. Competition may be introduced to liven the pace by recognizing the champion for each period in each exercise. These exercises are given three times a week on alternate days, as is the weight training program. In order to avoid overexertion and attendant muscle soreness at the start, the total exercise program may be accomplished in progressive steps. Three periods should be spent before the all-out effort is reached in time and innings.

Because of the great intensity of this program, it is always

BASKETBALL CONDITION RECORD												
Name_____						Season of _____						
Date	1	2	3	4	5	6	7	8	9	10	Sit Ups	Push Ups

conducted at the end of practice. The deadening effect of the pressure on the nerve endings in the finger tips would adversely affect shooting results if the push-ups were to be given before practice.

Only twelve to fifteen minutes are required to administer these three exercises, but the value in building endurance is worth more than two hours of scrimmage. The time saved is thus quite evident. Scrimmages can be used solely for coordinating team movements, determining the player combinations, and getting competitive experience.

It can be seen from the foregoing that much time and effort has been wasted in the past in conducting conditioning exercises. In many instances progress has been retarded by the procedures followed by many coaches. Since time is limited in the school situation, every coach should be alert to adopt methods which will produce the best results in the shortest possible time. Time saved in conditioning can be utilized profitably in other aspects of coaching.

The standards set for these exercises can be reached in four weeks. As a consequence, the program need not be continued longer than the first month of practice. Many high school coaches have reported that their players reach these standards so easily that they plan to raise the standards.

MAINTENANCE OF CONDITION

Fear that players will not stay in condition if exercises are not continued throughout the season has been raised by many coaches. They also worry about their players going stale if they are brought to their peak too soon. There is no evidence to support either of these concerns.

Ness and Sharos,[5] after conducting a weight training program for four weeks before the practice season began, checked the

---

[5] Phil Ness and Charles Sharos, "The Effect of Weight Training on Leg Strength and Vertical Jump" (Master's thesis, Springfield College, 1955).

players who had made a place on the varsity squad at the end of the season and found that each retained his jumping ability and leg strength at exactly the level at which he concluded his training program. The author has given the endurance tests to his squad at the end of the season, and has found that each player had maintained the standard attained at the end of the four-week training period prior to the beginning of the season. According to Steinhaus,[6] one can maintain his physical condition by ten seconds of activity per week at the level at which exercises were discontinued. A muscle under extreme stretch for that short a period will continue to retain its tone. It should be evident, therefore, that the requirements of playing games, to say nothing of practice periods, are more than enough to keep a team fit. On the contrary, the implications here suggest a cessation of practice once a team is well organized and playing smoothly. The reader is referred to Chapter 9 on Program of Practice for additional comments along this line.

STALENESS

Staleness is a much maligned word in sports, and is usually applied incorrectly in most instances. Coaches think of players' developing physical staleness from overwork, but there is little evidence to support such a thought. So long as a player maintains his weight after reaching the desired level of condition and gets sufficient rest and enough food, there is no possibility of physical staleness. Hard work never hurt anyone provided he attained the strenuous level by stages.

There is, however, such a thing as mental staleness—listlessness. This is brought about as the result of an inner revolt against the humdrum routine and regimentation of practice and the continued drive and pressure from the coach. This condition is not peculiar to sports but to all walks of life. The best antidote

---

[6] Arthur Steinhaus, *How to Keep Fit and Like It* (Chicago, Dartnell Press, 1957).

is a vacation, to permit a release of tension. Losing teams as well as winning teams face the same problem. As a consequence, the wise coach will plan for relief from practice for his players after mid-season. Such a procedure is indicated whether the team is winning or losing. See Chapter 9 on Program of Practice for examples of the salutary effect of these procedures.

SUMMARY

In summary, the points on conditioning may be stated as follows:

1. Conditioning means building strength and endurance.
2. Strength involves building muscle and is accomplished by the application of the principles of overload and intermittency.
3. Endurance is attained by applying the principles of intensity, repetition and intermittency.
4. Short, intense periods three times per week on alternate days produce best results.
5. Subject should reach desired level of condition as soon as possible (four to five weeks at beginning of season is sufficient).
6. Conditioning exercises should be conducted at the end of practice.
7. Suggested exercises are: weight training, spot running, sit-ups, and push-ups on finger tips.

9

PROGRAM OF PRACTICE

The answers to two penetrating questions will reveal the program of practice which each coach will adopt. But, whether or not the program is an intelligent, efficient one will depend on whether or not it will stand the test of certain guiding principles. It is the purpose of this chapter, first, to present these questions and the guiding principles, and then to lay out a sample program of practice as a means of demonstrating answers to the questions and showing the implementation of the guiding principles.

QUESTIONS

The first question one needs to ask himself is, "How do you plan to have your team play?" Each coach has his own philosophy about what system of play is most effective. Each has his own theories about shooting, pivoting, dribbling, passing, cutting, screening, guarding, offensive patterns, and defense. Some coaches use a definite system regardless of material, and adapt the material to the system. Others plan the style of play to fit the players. Others try to change from game to game in order to fit the play to the opponent. It is not the purpose here to discuss the efficacy of each of these systems or plans. Rather, it is to say that regardless of the plan each must determine in advance what plan he shall follow. Because the types of drills and other practice procedures which will be used will be determined by this decision, no organized procedure can be laid out until a definite plan has been adopted. Much time will be wasted in aimless activity and floundering around until this question is answered satisfactorily. Since time is a very important factor in the school situation, it is imperative that it be considered if the most is to be accomplished in the time available. It is always the cry of coaches that they do not have enough time to get their teams ready for competition. Before voicing such a complaint, one should check first to see if he has utilized his time most effectively. The first step in this direction is to make the decisions which are necessary to answer the first question.

The second question is, "How do you expect to carry out your plan?" The answer to this question involves, first, the over-all philosophy of the coach with respect to practice and preparing a team for a season of play. There are those who devote most of their time throughout the season to scrimmage. Their teaching consists of interrupting play from time to time to direct the movements of the players. The scrimmage is used as a means of conditioning, of selecting players, and of developing offense and defense, in lieu of fundamental drills. This procedure is followed day after day for the entire season.

Other coaches use scrimmage only as a means of coordinating team movements. Most of their practice time is devoted to half-court team drills and to group and individual fundamental drills. Their conditioning activities are a special part of their program of practice. This program is pursued throughout the season.

There are those who spend most of their time on fundamental drills. They work toward the perfection of the individual. Their practices are largely 2-man-3-man-4-man drills.

Others follow a meticulous time plan each practice. This plan varies as the season progresses, as competition starts, and regardless of the caliber of the team.

Ideally, each coach should determine exactly how he expects to prepare his team for competition and then follow that plan. Again, the factor of time must be considered.

PLANNING THE PRACTICE

The author has formed the habit of using a small, pocket-size, bound notebook for the purpose of recording his program of practice. At the end of each season, an analysis is made of the season's play for the purpose of guiding the planning for the following season. Strengths and weaknesses are noted in the team play, and these suggest needs for emphasis in practice for the next season. The observations and results during the season often suggest types of offense and defense that ought to be developed.

Players are evaluated, from which adaptations in play are suggested. On the basis of the personnel available for the coming season, a prognosis of those who are most likely to win places on the squad is made. This rarely turns out exactly as predicted, but it forms a basis from which to start when team organization begins. The rate of maturation of players between seasons never fails to bring many pleasant surprises. Occasionally, of course, some players remain static and others retrogress. It is easier, however, to spot these changes when one has a tentative rating setup as a guide. All these points are recorded.

The practice of planning in advance not only assures one of a well organized practice, but it makes it possible to get much more accomplished in the time available. Even though practice schedules are made out well in advance, one should always review his schedule before each practice. There should be no hesitancy in making changes which seem justified in the light of the results of a previous practice and on the basis of the progress which the squad is making. Nor should one hesitate to alter his plan during a practice if his observations indicate that more can be accomplished by some change. One should not be a slave to a plan.

LAWS OF LEARNING
APPLIED TO PRACTICE

The laws of learning should be the guiding principles which the coach uses to obtain the best results in the shortest time. These are time-tested principles which form the basis for sound and lasting learning. They are listed and discussed here to demonstrate the plan of implementation in the daily practice and in the practices at different stages during the season.

1. Players learn better if they have an understanding of the relationship of one phase of the pattern of play to another. As a consequence, the players should have the plan of play explained to them at the beginning of the season so that they may see and understand the goal toward which they are working. The first meeting of the squad for the season is the ideal time to lay out the plans for the season.

2. Players must have the will to learn. Without real desire, not much learning takes place; but, with real desire, almost anything is possible.

It is important to build this desire, eagerness, and enthusiasm and to take steps to maintain it throughout the season. This can be done by intelligent program planning. Such a plan will be discussed and demonstrated later in this chapter.

3. The whole-part plan of practice is most effective. The best advice from educational psychologists indicates that one should use a combination of the whole and the part method of teaching in order to obtain the most effective learning in sports. One must get a thorough grounding in individual techniques and also receive training in working as a part of a team. There is evidence to indicate that if one were to use, on the one hand, solely the team play as a means of practice, and on the other hand, only drills for perfecting individual techniques, a stronger team would develop in time by the use of the team-play (whole) method of practice. A combination of the two, however, produces the best results of all. As one plans his practices, he should, therefore, keep this point in mind.

4. One must drill repeatedly until perfection is attained. This is another way of saying one learns by doing under proper supervision. One interpretation of the Gestalt psychology has maintained that if one has a thorough understanding of a technique, it can be executed perfectly the first time. This principle is undoubtedly true, but evidently the transfer of ideas from the coach to the player has its shortcomings; because there is rarely a perfect performance with the first practice. As a consequence, repetition is necessary.

If one fails to repeat the practice of drills and team patterns, not only does he fail to improve, but he forgets much of what he learned. In general, 50 per cent of what is learned is forgotten within twenty-four hours. Within two weeks, no more than 10 per cent would be retained. On the basis of these facts, it is wise to plan practices so that learning progresses with as little retrogression as possible. One should repeat without fail the same drills the day following their introduction. The amount of repetition thereafter will depend on the clarity of presentation by the coach, his ability to observe and correct errors in performance, and the adeptness of the players in developing skills.

Learning takes place more effectively when drills are practiced in several short periods rather than in a few long periods. After a high degree of perfection is reached, short review practices of techniques every two or three weeks will suffice to maintain the level originally attained. As a consequence, if time permits before the first game, a whole week of practice which, daily, repeats the program of the first day and adds additional drills will produce the best results. The program which follows illustrates this plan.

5. There is a point at which improvement seems to stop or at least slow down. When this happens, one has reached a plateau in his development. Continued drill and coaching at this point are of little value and may be detrimental. The individual needs time to mature, to reflect upon and absorb the coaching he has received. The player will appear to be marking time, and then,

suddenly, he begins to move forward again. These plateaus occur periodically as one progresses. It is a wise coach who becomes aware of these stages and who regulates and changes his practice program accordingly.

There is a tendency, when a team is losing, to practice longer and harder with the hope of smoothing out its play. The chances are greater that the losing record will be aggravated and the efforts of the players will become more futile. Much more satisfactory results will, as a rule, be attained if the opposite tactics are practiced—if practice is shortened and made less strenuous; practice can even be cancelled with profit. Examples establishing this fact are legion. Some of the best performances of a team have occurred after a layoff.

Recently, a high school team won its right to enter the state tournament, which was to begin ten days after the last game of the regular season. The coach was at a loss to know what to do with his squad until tournament time. When it was suggested that he call off practice for a week and then work lightly just before the tournament, he was horrified; but he reluctantly followed the suggestion. His team played better and with greater enthusiasm in the tournament than at any time during the season, and they won the championship with ease. There was little more for the players to learn that season, but the layoff refreshed them beyond measure by relieving them of the monotony of continued practice.

There are those who feel that the tempo of practice must be maintained throughout the season in order to maintain condition. They fail to realize that once a level of condition is attained, the playing of games each week is more than sufficient to maintain top condition.

THREE STAGES OF PRACTICE

Implicit in the foregoing is the fact that, for the best results, the amount, type, and strenuousness of practice should vary at different stages during the season. Roughly speaking, there are three stages to the practice program. Exact dates cannot be set for these stages because conditions are never the same. The coach must be alert to observe the onset of listlessness, lack of progress, or loss of enthusiasm so that he may alter his practice program accordingly.

In general, with due regard for the protection of the feet of the players, the heaviest and most strenuous practice can be carried on with good results at the beginning of the pre-season period, before competition starts and before the squad is selected. Enthusiasm and desire are at a high pitch at this stage, and competition for places keeps every player eager. This period will last from two to six weeks depending upon the time available before the league or conference season begins. Top condition needed to carry a squad through a strenuous season is not reached until after four or six weeks of practice.

The pressure of competition requires that after the league or conference season begins there should be a lightening of the practice program. The preparation for specific games requires a definite change in the program. This is the second stage.

The third stage takes place after the season is half over. Practice can be lightened more than during the second stage. Cancellation of practice altogether, at least for those players who are doing most of the playing, will affect them like a spring tonic and help to keep their enthusiasm and level of performance at a high point. If games are played on Friday and Saturday, practice on Monday, and, late in the season, on Monday and Tuesday, may be cancelled with profit. It is surprising what recreative powers relief from practice produces. During these rest days the coach may desire to work with those players who are not getting to play in order to keep their development apace with their first teammates. These reserves are getting their rest by lack of play. The fact that the coach gives them his undivided attention is in itself a motivating factor for them.

6. Finally, the use of various teaching devices to enhance learning should not be overlooked. Of these, the motion picture film is probably the most effective. Taking motion pictures of

games and then analyzing them to determine individual and team strengths is most valuable. The actual record of play projected before the eyes removes all doubt and opinion and establishes the facts concerning performances. Going over these films with the players is a most convincing and tremendously enlightening procedure. In addition, it is possible to analyze the play of the opponent with great profit.

By the use of motion picture films of games, the coach is able to get across to players the effectiveness of techniques and patterns of play when repeated explanations and demonstrations have been to no avail. Many people learn better through visual means than auditory means; therefore, the visual approach to learning should not be neglected.

The use of motion pictures of the offensive and defensive systems and the fundamental drills to be used is an excellent supplement to other coaching methods. Greater uniformity of play and speed in learning are effected by this use of film.

Loop films for teaching techniques and plays have tremendous possibilities, but they have not been exploited to the extent they deserve. The particular value of a loop film is that it can be repeated continuously so that players may study each little detail. Loop film also permits the focus of attention on one particular technique or play.

Placing dittoed or mimeographed materials in the hands of the players permits them to study aspects of the game at their leisure. The fact that they have a printed record of the material which was demonstrated on the court permits each player to review these materials independently. Some players do not grasp a situation as quickly as others when it is demonstrated on the court, and often are reluctant to ask questions. The printed material permits them to catch up on their own initiative.

Some coaches are reluctant to place their ideas in writing for fear they may fall into the hands of their opponents and thus boomerang. The danger of this is rather remote and probably of little consequence if it should occur. Actually, one is a bit naive to think that there are any secrets about sports, or that any one individual has a monopoly on basketball information. Some utilize the available information more effectively than others. Putting one's thoughts and plans in writing has two values. It is an aid to the players, as already stated. It also helps the coach to clarify his own thinking and causes him to be more definite and specific which, in turn, helps the players to understand better what he wants them to do.

In Chapter 11, reference has been made to the use of condensed scouting reports in order to get before the players the important points upon which they should concentrate in meeting a particular opponent. This is another application of printed materials.

A helpful teaching device that has been on the market for some time is the strategy board. It can be used for problem solving, squad participation in review of play situations,, and in making blackboard demonstrations more realistic. It will be referred to again in Chapter 11.

DIVISIONS OF PRACTICE

Before giving examples of programs of practice, it may be helpful to the reader if the divisions of practice are presented. The various aspects of practice can be distributed rather logically under five divisions: (a) Preliminary or warm-up, (b) Drills, (c) Team Play, (d) Conditioning, and (e) Lecture.

Preliminary or Warm-up. It is seldom that all players arrive on the court at the same time. Only at institutions where the students are highly regimented would it be possible to have every player ready to practice at the same moment. As a consequence, there is time at the beginning of each practice when squad organization is not possible. This time can be used for working with individuals on their special needs. Players may be directed to practice individual techniques in which they are least proficient. This is a period which the coach can use informally for giving a player encouragement or advice, complimenting him, getting better acquainted with him, or discussing school problems.

This is a more casual period of practice when the players, for the most part, are free to work on their own. They always get in good shooting practice at this time. Generally speaking, the time spent in this phase of practice does not exceed twenty minutes. Since the author does not feel that calisthenics are a necessary part of basketball, individual practice using actual basketball situations is the means used for warming up. However, later in the season and particularly before games, as much as three-fourths to all of a practice period may be devoted to this type of practice. Informal shooting contests are devised. It becomes a period of relaxation and fun, but, at the same time, valuable shooting practice is obtained.

Drills. This part of the practice is devoted to learning individual and group techniques through formal drills. These drills should consist of parts of the team play to be used. Thus, while techniques are being stressed, parts of the team play are being learned incidentally. These drills include shooting, passing, pivoting, foot-work, rebounding, guarding, switching, stealing the ball, intercepting, double teaming, screening—all types of fundamentals to be used by the team. Many drills are diagrammed and explained in Volume Two of this series of publications. However, the coach may create drills which fit his pattern of play and which emphasize the points he desires to stress.

Based on a two-hour period and a four-week, pre-season practice, the drill period should consume at least half of the practice time during the first two weeks. This time will be reduced thereafter to not more than one-fourth of the practice time. When competition begins, periodical review of those fundamentals which, on the basis of play, need to be stressed is all that is required in drill practice. This may mean that once or twice a week short periods of practice of drills will be scheduled. There must always be some review of fundamentals throughout the season to correct careless habits which develop. The frequency of the drills must be determined by the observed need.

Team Play. In order that fundamental drills will have more meaning to the players, it is desirable to introduce some team play at the first practice. The players can see the relationship of the drills which they are practicing to the team play if they know what type of offense and defense is to be used. As a consequence, the players are given a taste of team play the very first day.

Based on a two-hour period and a four-week, pre-season practice, not more than thirty minutes per day would be devoted to team play during the first two weeks. Thereafter, this time would be increased to at least one hour. Even more time will be devoted to team play after competition begins and as emphasis is being given to meeting the particular type of play of an opponent.

At first, no opposition should be used in practicing team play. The emphasis at first is in coordinating the movements of players and perfecting sequence of movements of players with the ball. This cannot be accomplished while the players are learning movements if they must also be concerned with opponents. One desires to develop the confidence of the players in the plan of play, and this can be done best without opposition until the movement is learned.

As soon as the players begin to perform smoothly as a team, passive and controlled resistance should be introduced. Then, finally, the strongest opposition possible should be introduced. This last phase will be reached not later than one week before the first game and preferably two weeks before.

The fast break may be used as an example of this procedure in developing this phase of the offense. First, the movement of the fast break under the various rebound conditions is demonstrated. The squad then works by teams in practicing the movement. As the squad becomes familiar with the movement, one defensive player is put against the team with permission to do anything he pleases in an attempt to get the ball or stop the fast break. The opposition is then increased to two and finally to three. Since the object of the fast break is to outnumber the defense and thus get a scoring chance before the opponents have full strength on defense, there is no point in using more than three opponents. These three will create all the problems that might be encountered. If more than three players are used on defense, play becomes a full or half-court scrimmage. This is a phase of offense which should be stressed during another aspect of practice.

Except as a means of sorting out players, one should not attempt full-court scrimmage until the teams have become well coordinated in the various aspects of their team play. Rather, much time should be devoted to half-court work under controlled conditions. Except for pressing tactics and the fast break movement, most team play takes place in one half of the court.

Conditioning. Conditioning, as described in Chapter 8, is a four- or five-week program. It should be carried out at the beginning of the practice season. Not more than fifteen minutes per period is required for this program. Once the players meet the standards set for them, this division of practice is no longer included in the schedule.

The weight training program, because of its individual nature, must be conducted outside practice hours, so it is not included as a part of the time of regular practice. Usually, it is concluded before pre-season practice begins.

Lecture. Lecture is listed as a separate division of practice, even though lecture is interspersed throughout most practices in a greater or lesser degree. It is desired to give particular emphasis to the first meeting of the squad and to meetings during the competitive season when pictures of games are being studied and scouting reports are being given. At these times, the squad usually meets away from the playing court. Thus, lecture as connoted here is distinguished from the brief explanations that interrupt practice momentarily. When lecture periods are introduced, they take the time normally used for warmup, drill, or team play, or all or parts of the three divisions.

The first meeting of the squad at the beginning of the season should always be a lecture meeting. At this meeting, several routine matters must be handled: a schedule for physical examinations must be made, eligibility blanks filled out, the practice hours announced, the schedule presented, the training rules explained, the size of squad to be selected and the plan of selection explained, precautions for protecting the feet and ankles given, arrangements for checking out equipment made, and the general plan of play for the season discussed.

SAMPLE PROGRAMS

Bradley[1] studied the pre-season practice schedules of 180 Kentucky high schools. The following table is a composite of his findings. It will be noted that there are many similarities between this schedule and the one discussed in this chapter.

Questionnaire
on
A Study of the Organization of Pre-season
Basketball Practice

The purpose of this study is to determine the general pattern of organization of pre-season basketball practice in four hundred and seventy-one Kentucky high schools. In order to accomplish this, we would like you to estimate to the best of your ability and record approximately how much time you devote each day to the following:

1. Conditioning Drills
   These are general warmup exercises where no basketball is used and may include: calisthenics, running, medicine ball activity, push-ups, and so forth.

2. Fundamental Drills
   These drills include every skill fundamental to the game and include: dribbling, shooting, guarding, and passing.

---

[1] Carrol Bradley, "A Study of the Organization of Pre-season Basketball Practice Among Kentucky High Schools" (Master's thesis, Springfield College, 1953).

COMPOSITE TABLE SHOWING HOW 180 KENTUCKY HIGH SCHOOL BASKETBALL COACHES DIVIDED THEIR TIME DURING THE FIRST, SECOND, THIRD, AND FOURTH WEEKS OF PRE-SEASON PRACTICE, ACCORDING TO THE MEDIAN TIME FOR EACH DAY *

	Conditioning Drills	Fundamental Drills	Offensive Team Play			Defensive Team-Play	Lectures	Total
			No Defense	Tight Defense	Full Scrimmage			
First Week								
Monday	20	45	0	0	0	0	15	80
Tuesday	20	45	0	0	0	0	15	80
Wednesday	20	45	0	0	0	0	15	80
Thursday	20	40	0	0	0	0	0	70
Friday	20	40	0	0	0	0	5	75
Second Week								
Monday	15	40	15	0	0	0	10	80
Tuesday	15	40	10	0	0	0	10	75
Wednesday	15	40	10	0	0	0	10	75
Thursday	15	30	10	0	0	0	10	65
Friday	15	30	10	0	0	0	10	65
Third Week								
Monday	15	30	10	10	0	10	10	85
Tuesday	15	30	15	10	0	10	15	85
Wednesday	15	30	10	10	10	15	10	100
Thursday	10	30	15	10	0	10	10	85
Friday	15	30	10	10	10	10	10	95
Fourth Week								
Monday	10	30	10	10	10	15	10	95
Tuesday	10	30	10	15	15	15	5	100
Wednesday	10	30	10	10	15	15	5	95
Thursday	10	30	10	10	15	15	10	110
Friday	10	30	10	10	30	10	10	110

* "A Study of the Organization of Pre-season Basketball Practice Among Kentucky High Schools," Carrol Bradley, Springfield College, 1953.

94

3. Offensive Team Play

This phase of practice is concerned with practicing plays and testing them against a defensive team. This phase is usually carried out in the following manner:

   A. Against a "dummy defense" or no defense at all
   B. Against a tight defense
   C. Full-scale scrimmage.

4. Defensive Team Play

This next phase is concerned with practicing and testing defensive systems and strategy against offensive maneuvers. This would include: man-for-man and team (zone) defense.

5. Lectures

This phase concerns discussion of rules, strategy and tactics, and explanations of new plays and defenses.

The following example of the first four weeks of a practice season is a plan that was organized before practice began and was carried out with very little alteration. The schedule was predicated on the basis that all but two of the squad of the previous year were returning, that the starting line-up of the past season was intact, that only three candidates unfamiliar with the system of play would be competing for places, and on the basis of an analysis of play for the past season and prognosis of the type of personnel and competition which would be met. It is also based on the fact that the plan of play for the season would include pressing tactics, team defense, fast break, free lance, continuity, and screen offense; that practice drills should stress rebounding, "blocking" out, 1 on 1, 2 on 2, switching, 2 on 1, 3 on 2, pivoting, stealing the ball, interceptions, double teaming, playing in front of the pivot, free throwing, shooting, and conditioning. It was also decided that, contrary to past practices, offense would be stressed first. No specific time schedule is indicated but the plan which is discussed on the foregoing pages was followed.

1. *First Practice Session*

Meeting in classroom to organize for season
Physical examinations

Eligibility
Practice hours
Checking equipment
Training rules
Plan for picking the squad
Schedule of games
Plan of play

2. *Second Practice Session*
Shooting informally
Lay-up drill
Squads of four
Rebounding
Continuity
Fast break
Free throws

3. *Third Practice Session*
Repeat 2.
Conditioning

4. *Fourth Practice Session*
Same as 2. plus screens

5. *Fifth Practice Session*
Same as 4.
Conditioning

6. *Sixth Practice Session*
Shooting—field and free
Stealing ball
1 on 1
2 on 2
2 on 1
3 on 2
Pressing defense

7. *Seventh Practice Session*
Same as 6.
Conditioning

8. *Eighth Practice Session*
Same as 6.
Add team defense

9. *Ninth Practice Session*
   Same as 8.
   Conditioning

10. *Tenth Practice Session*
    Same as 8.

11. *Eleventh Practice Session*
    Warmup
    Fast break drill
    Continuity drill against defense with fast break
    Conditioning

12. *Twelfth Practice Session*
    Warmup
    Stealing ball
    Double teaming
    Press after free throw or field goal

13. *Thirteenth Practice Session*
    Warmup with free throws
    Scrimmage with no press
    Conditioning

14. *Fourteenth Practice Session*
    Warmup with free throws
    Scrimmage with press

15. *Fifteenth Practice Session*
    Warmup with free throws
    Scrimmage
    Conditioning

16. *Sixteenth, Seventeenth, Eighteenth, Nineteenth, Twentieth Practice Sessions*
    Warmup—field and free-throw shooting
    Review different drills each day
    Scrimmage each day with different combinations to select
       squad and get starting line-up
    Conditioning on odd days.

Another example of a pre-season practice schedule is shown below. This schedule is based upon the same conditions as the foregoing one. It is developed on a specific time basis and is organized for continuous use. The schedule for one day is adaptable for any day.

1. *SHOOTING*—3:00 to 3:30

    Work alone or in pairs. Start in close. Shoot from all spots. Develop a two-hand shot for outside shots. For half the period, practice following all shots. Get your free-throw practice during this period. During each shooting period the shots of some will be charted. (This is for motivation purposes.)

2. *THREE LINE DRILL*—3:30 to 3:40

    Alternate days use two-line drill with dribble, changing direction before drive.

3. *SQUADS OF FOUR* (4)—3:40 to 3:50

    Alternate days—1 on 1 and 2 on 2 drills will be used.

4. *REBOUND FOR PROTECTION AND STEALING BALL* —3:50 to 4:00

    Alternate days—2 on 1 and 3 on 2 drills will be used.

5. *FAST-BREAK DRILL*—4:00 to 4:20

    With and without opposition.

6. *CONTINUITY AND PLAY PRACTICE*—4:20 to 4:40

    Use center as screener-feeder and rebounder, primarily. Periods 5 and 6 will also be used for team defense pressing tactics, etc.

7. *CONDITIONING EXERCISES ON M. W. F.*—4:40 to 5:00

    T and Th will be used for special drills and scrimmage.

NOTE: After first week, scrimmages will be held on Tuesday and Thursday after shooting period. Candidates will be divided into teams for team play and scrimmage. Squad will be chosen not later than Nov. 19. This date is based on a beginning practice date of Oct. 15. Choices will be based upon individual ratings and rating as a member of a team.

10

PICKING THE TEAM

The most difficult and yet the most vital job of a coach is the selection of the players for his team and squad. Every coach wants to play the five boys who will produce a winning team. Also, he wants support for these five when they need relief or replacement. He must have scoring power, ball-handling ability, rebound strength, and defense; he needs speed and height; he is looking for boys with the desire to sacrifice for the team, boys who are competitive. He must weigh experience and judgment against the potential and initiative of youth. He is certainly not concerned about race, religion, or nationality. Rather, his job is to find the happy combination of characteristics that will produce a smooth-playing, effective unit. Seldom do five players or a squad possess all the characteristics a coach hopes to find. Therefore, the task of detecting hidden talents, of recognizing their presence and then developing them to the optimum of their potential becomes his major concern. Just how is this done?

Some coaches seem to have an innate capacity for discovering talent and molding it into a smooth-working team. Years of experience have helped them to develop the art of successful selection of personnel. But if they were asked to describe the process or write down their criteria for others to follow, they would probably be at a loss to comply. It is an inexplainable art with them, like grandmother's art of cooking. She had no recipes, she merely put in a little of this and a little of that. She couldn't tell you how much and you couldn't duplicate the dish, but it was a tasty product that she turned out.

GUIDING PRINCIPLES

An attempt will be made here to present some guiding principles for selecting players, to indicate and weigh desirable qualities, to outline procedures by which these qualities may be observed, to suggest and point out the value and use of recorded data of various kinds, and finally to differentiate between qualities that are the result of teaching and practice, and those which are more or less inherent. The purpose here is to be as helpful as possible to the inexperienced coach so that he may learn vicariously what others have learned through years of experience.

Those who recruit their teams are just as much in need of definite and reliable criteria to guide their selections as those who experience the thrill and satisfaction of molding their teams from the boys who report for play on their own initiative and desire to be a member of a team.

1. Reaction Time

Without question the most outstanding characteristic or quality, which is not only desired in a basketball player but necessary for successful all-round performance, is reaction time. Basketball is not so much a game of moving over long distances in a short time as it is a game of quickness—quickness in starting; quickness in stopping; quickness in changing direction; quickness in thrusting out with the hand or stepping with the foot. A fraction-of-a-second advantage over an opponent in getting to a desired position is the difference between outmaneuvering or being outmaneuvered.

Reaction time in its isolated sense is that time which elapses between a given signal and the beginning of the initial responses to that signal. In a practical sense, in basketball, interest is centered in both the reaction time plus the time required for the primary move. Thus, reaction-performance time becomes a practical consideration. The latter is a learned quality which will improve with practice and the use of the most effective and efficient techniques. The former is an inherited characteristic similar to the I.Q. Practice, training, or conditioning does not affect the measurable results significantly.[1] The ultimate potential of a player is determined, therefore, from the measure of his reaction time rather than from an observation of his present performance.

The importance of this point should be self-evident. At a given time one boy may easily outperform another, but with practice the boy with the better reaction time will eventually demonstrate his superiority. If one is choosing players for immediate results, then, of course, he will choose those who demonstrate superior performance at that moment. Continued success in coaching is predicated on continued progress. Therefore, one must always look ahead. The boy who demonstrates a marked superiority in reaction but an inferiority, at the moment, in performance should not be eliminated. Rather, he should receive the concentrated efforts of the coach because he is most likely to become the great player.

Some years ago a boy was eliminated from the squad of the great Phog Allen because he did not measure up to the others in performance, though he was one of the quickest boys on the squad. He knew he did not rate a position on the squad at that moment, but he had a great desire to play; so he asked his coach what was wrong with his play in order to work to improve. The words of Dr. Allen still ring in my ears: "Everything is wrong with your play, but if you are willing to work on fundamentals you have great potential and may make it in a year or two." That

---

[1] James Genasci, "A Study of the Effect of Participation in Physical Education Activities and Athletics on Reaction and Movement Time" (Doctoral dissertation, Colorado State College, 1960).

boy wanted to make it, so he worked unceasingly; and in his senior year he was a star on the Kansas team and an all-conference selection.

That boy had quick reaction time. All he needed was an opportunity to learn techniques. Agility and coordination must be stressed, but they are learned qualities. A boy with quick reactions has no difficulty, under intelligent supervision, in developing them; because with quick reaction he already has the potential.

In all my years of coaching I have never had a player make a first-team position who was not rated, on reaction time, among the first twenty candidates reporting for the team. On many occasions the freshmen candidates, from 60 to 100 in number, have been rated in order of their reactions. These results have been kept until all had graduated and then compared with the squad rosters. Never has a boy below the first 20 made the squad.

Several devices may be used to measure reaction. The most accurate is to use an electrical timing device similar to the Hale [2] reaction-performance timer. This is rather expensive, but if one is fortunate enough to have such a timer, very accurate measurements may be obtained.

The reaction time varies for different muscle groups. The larger the muscle the slower the reaction. The arm and hand reactions are usually faster than the leg and foot reactions. Total body reaction will be slower than the reaction of either the hand or the foot. A combination of foot and hand reaction or total body reaction will give a more useful measure for basketball rating purposes. A heel lifting movement, as devised by Genasci,[3] provides an excellent method for measuring total body reaction. Figure 4, p. 103, shows the plan for this procedure.

Arm and hand reaction and leg and foot reaction can be determined by using types of movements related to basketball.

---

[2] Franklin Henry, "Precision and Operation of the Hundredth-Second Electric Timer," *Research Quarterly,* March 1959, p. 117.

[3] Genasci, *op. cit.*

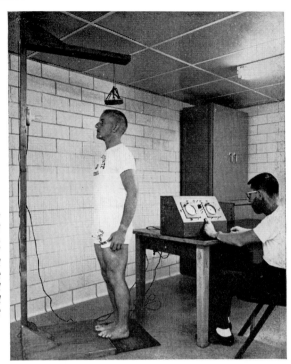

Figure 4. *Apparatus for measuring total body reaction. Subject in "ready" position for heel lift when l i g h t flashes. When head touches suspended switch, clock at right is stopped.*

For example, arm and hand movements as used in guarding (in an attempt to block the ball) and leg and foot movements as used in stepping in one direction or another are excellent methods. Contrary to the beliefs of some, no significant difference has been found in arm and hand reactions in movements to the right or left or movements up or down. Figure 5, illustrating methods of measuring arm and hand and leg and foot reactions is shown on the following page.

Penny Cup Test. If one does not have an electrical or mechanical timing device available, he may use a stop watch and devise tests which crudely measure reaction and performance. A test which originated at Stanford University some years ago has been used with good results. The test was called the penny cup test, and it may be administered as described on p. 104.

Figure 5. *Switch arrangement for measuring reaction-performance time in foot movements. On signal, subject lifts foot from large black switch and touches small black switch to his left. Elapsed time from signal to lifting foot measures reaction. Elapsed time from signal to tripping small switch is reaction - performance time.*

Three one-pound coffee cans are placed on radial lines thirty feet from a starting point, and three feet apart. Each can is given a name, 1, 2, or 3, or red, white, or blue. A balk line is placed eight feet from the starting point. A contestant starts with his back to the cups and his toes even with the starting point. A penny is placed in his hand. For best performance he should crouch with knees bent to an angle of about 120° and with a bend at the waist. The feet should be spread about shoulder width with the weight evenly distributed on the feet.

The starting signal should be given in the same rhythmic cadence ready-set-go for each contestant so that maximum readiness may be obtained. The contestant must be stationary, not falling back, when the signal is given. At the signal "Go," a stop watch is started.

The contestant, for best results, should lean and step directly backward without raising his center of gravity. As he reaches the eight-foot balk line, the can into which he is to place the coin is called out. At this point he moves directly to the proper can and quickly drops the coin into the can. As the sound of the coin hitting the can is heard, the watch is stopped and the time recorded. To compensate for variations in time, fifteen repetitions of a set sequence should be given. The time for the fifteen repetitions is determined and this represents the record for the contestant. He should not throw the penny at the can in an attempt to gain time, because if the coin misses or does not remain in the can, the watch continues to run. Gambling in this manner will result in slower times.

While any sequence for the fifteen trials may be used, the same sequence should be used for each contestant in order to make the times comparable. A suggested sequence is: B-R-W-R-B-W-W-R-B-R-W-B-R-W-B. "B" stands for "Blue" or "1"; "R" stands for "Red" or "2"; and "W" stands for "White" or "3."

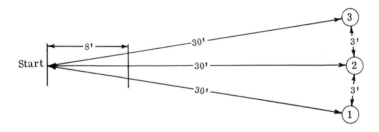

The distance from the starting point to the cans may be less than thirty feet, but should, of course, be the same for each contestant. Sufficient distance should be allowed so that the human error in operating the stop watch will not be too great a factor. If it is desired to reduce the time of administration, the best time out of three trials may be used; but this will not be the most valid measure.

Each contestant should be given an opportunity to practice so that he can familiarize himself with the technique and remove as much practice effect as possible.

Knox Test. Knox combined the penny cup test with several performance tests and produced some rather phenomenal results in predicting the personnel for each squad of an eight-team league, the team ratings in the league, ratings of the team in a post-season tournament, and the selections for an all-star team. His predictions were made before basketball practice started for the season. His personal selections were 80 per cent correct. His team standings for both the league play and the tournament were in error in only two instances. He picked correctly the winner and second-place teams. His all-star squad was 68 per cent correct.

The complete Knox battery consisted of a speed dribble test, wall bouncing test, dribble shoot test, penny cup test and foul shooting. The free-throw test was found to have no validity because of too few trials, so should not be included in the battery.

Cox modified the Knox test and built a test based entirely upon time. The items in his test and the instructions for administering the test are given in the next section. This test was used at Springfield College in Massachusetts for a number of years.

One might be inclined to conclude that small players would have an advantage over tall players in the test. The results, however, do not bear out such a conclusion. In one striking instance, the tallest and shortest candidates were just one-tenth of a second apart, and they were first and second in the ratings of sixty candidates.

The Cox Basketball Rating Tests. These comprise a series of fundamental skill tests devised by the author, and administered by Vernon W. Cox, Freshman Basketball Coach at Springfield College, to all freshman basketball candidates who report each season.

The tests are used to help the coach select players for the freshman and varsity squads.

The tests are designed to test various abilities of the players in the fundamental skills of basketball. These tests can determine a player's ability in speed, coordination in dribbling, passing and receiving, and his ability to respond to commands. They are administered after two weeks of practice on fundamentals and conditioning exercises.

Materials needed for testing:
7 obstacles (chairs served this purpose)
a basketball
a stop watch
3 tin cups
record sheet

The tests were given in the following order:
(a) Alternating Lay-Up Shot
(b) Wall Bounce Test
(c) Penny Cup Test
(d) Dribble Maze
(e) Stop and Pivot
(f) Dribble Shot Test

A brief description of each test follows. The following sequence was used for each test: explanation, demonstration, application.

(a) *Alternating Lay-Up Shot.* This test consists of ten alternating lay-up shots from beneath the basket. The following instructions are given to the subject before the test is started: "The purpose of this test is to see how fast you can make ten alternating lay-up shots. I will start the watch on the signal, 'go,' and I will stop the watch when you make the tenth basket. You may start on either side of the basket, but you will alternate each shot even though you lose control of the ball and it rolls away. You cannot go on until you have made a basket on one side." The instructor should then demonstrate the test and let the subject practice a few shots. "This is a test to see how fast you can make ten alternating lay-up shots."

(b) *Wall Bounce Test.* A line is marked on the floor five feet from the wall and parallel to it. The subject stands behind the wall, with heels on the floor, and bounces the ball against the wall fifteen times, as rapidly as possible. His score is the number of seconds the process requires.

Note: If any rebound is such that the subject has to take more than one step to recover it, the score is considered invalid and the test repeated. The following instructions are given to the subject before the test is administered: "The purpose of this test is to find out how long it will take you to bounce the ball against the wall fifteen times. You must keep bouncing the ball; I will count the number of times the ball hits the wall and tell you when to stop. Try it a few times and then wait for the starting signal which will be, 'ready, go.' I will start the watch with the signal 'go' and will stop it when the ball hits the wall the fifteenth time. Your score will be the number of seconds this requires."

(c) *Penny Cup Test*—Diagram of the set-up for this test:

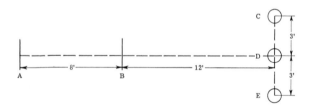

A—Starting Line; B—Signal Line; C—Red Tin Cup; D—White Tin Cup; E—Blue Tin Cup.

The subject stands on the starting line with his back to the cups; he has a penny in his hand. On the signal, 'go,' he turns and runs toward the cups. As he crosses the signal line he is given a direction signal by the starter; he continues to the cup indicated by the starter and places the penny in that cup. The direction signal is one of three words: "red," "white," or "blue." The time that elapses between the starting signal and the sound of the penny striking in the cup is measured with the stop watch. The process is repeated four times. The score is the sum of times required in the four repetitions. A stop watch that can be stopped and started again without having the hands return to zero makes it necessary to read the watch only once and eliminates the process of adding the four scores.

The following instructions were given to the subjects before the test: "Watch me! I stand on this line with a penny in my hand. Notice that my back is toward the cups and I am in a crouched position. At the signal 'go,' I turn and start toward the cups; as I cross the signal line, I hear the signal 'red,' and so I continue to the red cup and put the penny in it. If, as I crossed the signal line I had heard the signal, 'blue,' I would have gone to the blue cup. I want you to do the same thing, but do it as quickly as you can. The watch will start with the signal, 'go,' and will stop at the sound of the penny entering the cup. The watch will continue to run until the penny is in the cup. You will not be timed while you are returning to the starting line to repeat the test."

(d) *Dribble Maze*—A diagram of the set-up for this test:

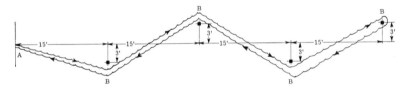

A—Starting Line; B—Obstacles (chairs–direction of progress).

The score in this test is obtained by the use of a stop watch. It consists of the time that elapses between the signal, 'go,' and the instant the subject recrosses the starting line.

The following instructions are given to the subjects before they start the test: "The purpose of this test is to find how long it will take you to dribble this basketball in a zig-zag course down and back by those four chairs. Watch me as I demonstrate this test. Notice that I place the ball on the starting line and stand behind it with my hands on my knees. With the signal, 'go,' I pick up the ball and start. Do not slow down until you have crossed the finish line. Your score will be the number of seconds it takes you to complete the test."

(e) *Stop and Pivot*

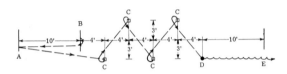

A—Wall; B—Starting Line; C—Obstacles (chairs); D—Ball; E—Center Court Line.

The following directions apply for this test: "Stand on the starting line facing down court. On the signal, 'go,' pivot, run to the wall, and touch it. Go to the first obstacle, stopping in a crouched position and placing the *left* foot on a small circle drawn next to the obstacle. Pivot on the *right* foot and go to the second obstacle. Stop with the *right* foot in a small circle drawn next to the second obstacle. Pivot on the *left* foot and go to the third obstacle, placing the *left* foot on the circle next to the third obstacle. Pivot on the *right* foot and go to the fourth obstacle. Place the *right* foot on the circle next to the fourth obstacle and pivot on the *left* foot. Finally, go to the basketball, pick it up, and dribble over the center line."

Caution subject to stand on starting line with hands on knees. This is a test of speed. The watch starts with the signal 'go,' and stops when the subject crosses the center line.

(f) *Dribble Shot Test*

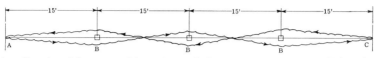

A—Starting Line; B—Obstacles (chairs); C—Basket; D—Direction of Progress.

The technique of this test is the same as that of the dribble maze test except that there are three obstacles instead of four. The subject dribbles a basketball through the maze and must make a basket before he returns. If he misses the shot for basket, he must keep shooting until he makes it. He may use any kind of shot he desires, but the one-handed lay-up is appropriate.

The following instructions and explanations are given to the subjects before the start of the test: "Start behind the starting line with your hands on your knees and the ball resting on the starting line. On the signal, 'go,' pick up the ball and dribble through the maze, shooting a basket on the other end and returning through the maze. When you start, be sure to go to the right of the first obstacle. This is so that you will approach the basket from the right side and thus will be in a better position to shoot. The watch will start with the signal, 'go,' and will stop when you cross the finish line. This is a test for speed, so don't slow down as you approach the finish line."

2. Height

Height is selected as the second quality to look for in the selection of personnel. It is a tangible quality which is easily determined and observed. Good, tall boys are a tremendous asset to a team for rebounding purposes and as a defensive deterrent around the basket. A tall boy is of greatest value if he has fast reactions, but the mere fact of height is always of great concern to an opponent. The psychological advantage is so great that it often demoralizes an opponent and causes the coach to reorganize his whole plan of attack.

Coaches, particularly on the high school level, should be slow to eliminate the tall boy. If he has fast reactions, he is worth all the time and effort devoted to him. It must be remembered that the big high school boy is going through the awkward stage and needs patient and persistent attention to develop his coordination and agility. Some do not begin to realize their potential, height, until college age or after.

Bill Russell of San Francisco University and later of the Boston Celtics is an example of the tall boy who rewarded the efforts of his coaches. Even as a member of an NCAA champion team, Russell was far from an agile, well coordinated player. He could not dribble and was seldom used as part of an offensive pattern. But as a watchdog of the basket on both offense and defense, he had no peer. His coaches were wise to concentrate on those aspects of his play in which he was most valuable to his team. Later, as a professional player, he developed and provided the Boston Celtics with the needed ingredient to make them a world-famous basketball power.

These comments are not intended to underrate the value of smaller players. There is always a place for the good small boy in basketball. His dash and spirit, clever floor maneuvers, and untiring efforts furnish the spark and color needed to make a great team. Present training methods have put so much added jump into the little man that he has become as spectacular at dunking the ball as his taller mate. However, every team needs some height and ruggedness to go with the shorter players. It is a credit to basketball that it is the one sport that has afforded an outlet for the tall boy. It has given him pride in himself and helped him to develop confidence at a time when he was self-conscious and thinking of himself as a freak because of his height.

There is always the question of how to proportion the short boys to the tall boys on a squad. This is a relative matter and many times a coach does not have any choice. Hobson, whose Oregon teams were the first to feature tall boys, had six in a squad of fifteen, six players who were 6′4″ and above. His team heights were 6′8″, 6′6″, 6′5″, 5′11″, and 5′8″. This team, which had perfect balance, has been used as a model; and it was the first NCAA champion.

Reaction time and height are tangible and constant qualities which are rather easy to measure. At the outset of the pre-season training period, the coach knows the degree of these qualities in his squad and plans his season according to the absence or presence of them. These, of course, are only a part of the qualities that he is looking for and needs in order to have a team of real competitors. The other qualities are less tangible and require his continued discerning observation and study to detect them in his candidates.

3. Desire

The foremost of these intangible qualities may best be identified by the word "desire." A boy who has this quality is one who is so eager to play and to win that he is continually striving for perfection of his own techniques and of the play of his team. His efforts are tireless, and he cannot tolerate mediocrity. He drives himself to attain top condition. He follows training rules to the letter. He places his team and his school above self. He is a tough competitor. This quality compensates for many shortcomings that he may have at the outset, because he'll strive to correct them; and he is a constant inspiration to his teammates.

4. Sport Intelligence

Next, a high degree of sport intelligence is necessary. Boys are required to make many instantaneous judgments during the course of a game. They are partly conditioned reflexes and partly strategic decisions based upon the analysis of the situation at a specific moment in the game. Some boys seem to have an innate sense of what to do, others acquire this ability rather quickly, and some can seldom be expected to select the right action even after extensive practice and playing experience.

5. Emotional Control

A high degree of emotional control is absolutely necessary for successful performance in a game which creates such a high degree of tension. A player who can maintain calmness at the most exciting moment, who can perform with as much relaxation and surety during a game as during a practice is the one who can be expected to come through at the crucial moment. He must not be disturbed or upset by adverse conditions, by apparent bad breaks, by officials' decisions, by hostile spectators, or by baiting or unsportsmanlike tactics of an opponent. If he can keep his head under vexing circumstances such as these, the effectiveness of his performance will not suffer. When he comes through in spite of these circumstances, he not only eliminates them, he silences the most critical and develops confidence and poise which strengthen him for subsequent similar situations. A player on a recent United States Olympic Basketball Team, who was heralded as one of the greatest players America has ever produced, was ineffectual during the Olympic games because of his loss of emotional control. Instead of reacting to what he considered bad officiating and rough opponents' tactics by increasing his efforts, he displayed fits of anger and unsportsmanlike conduct.

Occasionally, a boy will report for practice and impress the coach with his outstanding ability. He will execute the fundamentals perfectly, he will be unexcelled in scrimmage, and the coach may label him as his number one prospect. When this player is put into the line-up to start the first game, however, his performance is reversed. He commits violations, shoots wildly, and is generally disorganized. The coach is puzzled, but he concludes that the boy has "first game jitters." But the performance is repeated in the next game and in the next; and in spite of the coach's efforts to help him, his game performance does not improve. This is a case of the player's becoming too tense, too emotional in game competition. Some boys are unable to control their emotions or to perform under pressure, and this eliminates some very promising candidates.

6. Sportsmanship

Finally, a player must display unquestioned sportsmanship. Good sportsmanship is not a quality which is inherent in basketball or in any other sport for that matter, but it can be developed through proper leadership and example. The kind of sportsmanship a player has developed is clearly displayed during heated competition. Bad conduct not only marks the guilty player but also reflects adversely upon the coach and the institution which the player represents. Commendable conduct, on the other hand, wins the applause and respect of others and builds character for trusted citizenship.

METHODS OF RATING

How can a coach determine the degree to which these intangible qualities are possessed by each candidate for the team? The only reliable method is to keep a written record or log of each practice. This record consists of an anecdotal record of the observations of the behavior of each individual during all aspects of the practice. Such factors as promptness and regularity in reporting to practice, the extent to which a player works on his weaknesses during the informal part of the practice, the earnestness with which he practices, the extent and manner in which he works with his teammates, the reaction of his teammates toward him, his reaction to coaching, to criticism, to discipline, to adverse conditions, to pressure of competition, and his performance in handling various play situations all tend to reveal the individual. An accumulation of observations of this kind

INDIVIDUAL PERFORMANCE CHART

AT _____ VS _____ DATE _____

TEAM _____

Player's Name	SHOTS		GOALS		REBOUNDS			RECOVERIES		HELD BALL					FOULS	
	Field	Foul	Field	Foul	Def.	Off.	Assist	Interc.	Held Ball	Def.	Off.	Bad Pass	Fumbles	Violations	Pers.	Tech.
1.																
2.																
3.																
4.																
5.																
6.																
7.																
8.																
9.																
10.																
TOTAL																
AVERAGE																

TEAM _____

Player's Name	SHOTS		GOALS		REBOUNDS			RECOVERIES		HELD BALL					FOULS	
	Field	Foul	Field	Foul	Def.	Off.	Assist	Interc.	Held Ball	Def.	Off.	Bad Pass	Fumbles	Violations	Pers.	Tech.
1.																
2.																
3.																
4.																
5.																
6.																
7.																
8.																
9.																
10.																
TOTAL																
AVERAGE																

will, when tabulated and analyzed, tend to place the individual in a definite pattern so that he may be compared with his teammates.

In addition, statistical records should be kept of all practices and particularly of all scrimmages and games. This is a job for the managers to perform. They should be thoroughly instructed in this job in order to assure accurate records. Shooting records, both field and free shots, rebounds, assists, fouls, violations, bad passes, interceptions, recoveries, held balls permitted, held balls created, and stolen balls tend to show strengths and weaknesses of players. These statistics are also helpful to the players and suggest points of emphasis for subsequent practices. Forms for convenience in recording may be devised. Several forms for recording statistics are on the market, but each coach may design his own to fit his own particular needs. One kind of form is presented on page 116 as an example.

It is highly important that written records be kept. A coach can be easily misled by impressions made by isolated incidents. For example, a player may make a particularly brilliant play or he may fail to perform properly at an important point. The incident may impress itself so indelibly upon the mind of the coach that he tends to generalize about the performance of this player on the basis of this one incident. A study of records of the total performance may show that this impression is entirely erroneous and does not reflect the total performance of this player.

PRACTICE PROCEDURES FOR RATING PURPOSES

If a coach is faced with a large turnout of candidates, he may set up a plan of practice that will help him and his assistants to select those who are most nearly ready at that time to be given further consideration. The drills listed on p. 118 may be used in order that each player may be observed:

(1) Two-line formation for lay-up shots;

(2) Progressive shooting drill around the court at each available basket. The squad can be divided into as many groups as there are balls available. Each candidate shoots the designated shot at each basket in rotation until he makes the shot. A free throw, one-hand set, jump shot, or two-hand chest shot can be used at a designated distance from the goal;

(3) A two-line short passing drill up and down the court for observing ball handling and body control;

(4) A two-player short passing drill up and down the court with one player running backward, for rating ability to move backward quickly and at the same time to handle the ball;

(5) A dribble drill whereby players move left, right, backward, and forward at the direction of the coach, to note their ability to control the ball and to move in different directions while watching the coach for directions;

(6) A three-player, figure-of-eight weave up and down the court;

(7) Short periods of scrimmage to observe the performance of players in competition.

After a two-week period the coach will have accumulated helpful information to add to his other records for reducing his squad to a workable size. During this period of time many players will make a self-evaluation and eliminate themselves.

The process of selection should go on progressively. After each practice an evaluation and rating should take place. It has been found convenient to group candidates into three categories: those who are very impressive and, therefore, stand out during each practice; those who do not impress because of their apparent lack of talent—these also stand out; and those who go more or less unnoticed. The last group represents the "run of the mill" type of player. He does his job effectively but is not spectacular.

Those in the first and last groups are kept for further trial and observation; those in the second group, after careful consideration, are eliminated from further consideration. This process goes on from practice to practice until the squad is reduced to twenty or twenty-five. From this number the final selection of a squad of twelve is made. The remainder can be retained as a junior varsity squad for further development. Only sophomores and juniors should be retained on a junior varsity because they are the only ones who will be available the following season.

These procedures give everyone a fair chance and leave each with a feeling that he has been given consideration and an opportunity to measure his ability with that of others. If, in addition, the results of tests that have been given are posted, most criticism on the part of candidates is forestalled. They can make their own comparisons and see exactly how their performance rates with others. Certainly these procedures help the coach to discover the potential candidates for present and future teams and gives him a sense of confidence in his selections.

Finally, the coach should welcome and seek information from all sources. Other members of the faculty get insights into the personality, strength and weaknesses of the athletes who are in their classes. They are usually willing and eager to pass this information along to the coach. Fellow coaches can be helpful. Those who are deeply interested in sports and who follow the team closely volunteer their evaluations of the players. The academic and test records of all candidates should be studied carefully in order to identify weak and potentially weak students.

One should recognize that information from these sources can be helpful. It often gives the coach a new and different basis for understanding, evaluating, and helping his players. However, the coach should never be prejudiced or moved to action solely on the basis of such information. Every boy should be given a chance to prove himself.

11

COACHING AIDS

The coach should avail himself of numerous and varied devices for imparting his ideas to his players. In spite of the fact that he attempts to communicate at the players' level, he is not consistently successful in transferring his ideas to them, and his concepts are not always revealed in court action.

THE SPOKEN WORD

The spoken word is not always interpreted in the same way by all players. The jargon of the coach may not mean what he intends. For example, "to play a tight defense" means to one person to concentrate the defense about the goal; to another it means to play close to the player to whom one is assigned. The level of understanding and the basketball experience vary from player to player. The author once had the interesting experience of teaching basketball, through an interpreter, to Koreans. The job of choosing the right words to convey the intended ideas was a most challenging one. At first, as one eagerly awaited the outcome of directions being relayed through the interpreter, it was sometimes rather startling to observe the results. After a time, however, by trial and error, key words and phrases were discovered so that a common understanding was established. This experience emphasized the need for meeting the player at his level and adopting a verbal relationship which is mutually understood.

Actually, the Koreans were not different from Americans. The language barrier merely accentuated the problem of understanding. On one occasion, a very promising candidate seemed unable to grasp a rather fundamental defensive team technique of playing in front of the pivot. Repeated explanations failed to have any effect. Finally, during a scrimmage, the light of understanding suddenly dawned. After the scrimmage, when complimented on his play, the boy explained how he had discovered a unique technique of his own (the very same that had been dinned into his ears many times) for stopping the pivot man. Either words from the coach had not been meaningful, or the boy, at his level of basketball experience, was not ready for the idea.

THE WRITTEN WORD

The art of stating an idea so clearly that it is revealed, as intended, to another is attained only after concentrated effort. Often, too much is said, resulting in confusion rather than enlightenment. Every coach would profit by putting his thoughts and ideas into writing. This procedure would help in organizing his thinking and presentation into more logical, understandable form.

As an example, on one occasion the author was invited to coach a WAC basketball team in Europe. Because of other responsibilities which made it impossible to be present at practices, written instructions were provided for each practice after discussing with the group the results of the previous practice. In other words, the team was coached by "correspondence." This team worked diligently and followed instructions earnestly, and as a result, developed into a very smooth-working, successful team in accordance with the pattern of written instructions. The team won its way to the finals of the Eucom Tournament.

EXPLAINED DEMONSTRATION

Demonstration is a most effective method of teaching. However, merely to say, "this is the way, see?", and then go through the motions of a particular technique or pattern of play is not likely to be very revealing. One should explain each step in the demonstration so that the full significance of each sequence may be grasped. Much of the value of demonstration as a coaching device is lost unless the attention of the observer is directed to each important detail as the demonstrator performs.

The coach may act as a demonstrator if he is a highly skilled player who can give expert demonstrations. If he is not an able demonstrator himself, he should use his more outstanding and experienced players as demonstrators under his directions.

THE USE OF FILM

Motion pictures have proved to be one of the most effective coaching aids. Players seem to be sight-minded so that the showing of film with analytical comments can be a most valuable supplement to court practices.

There are many types of film. Pictures of one's own games are the best investment because their use is varied. In the first place, they give a permanent record of the play of opponents. Thus, they are an excellent means of scouting. The play of both the opponent and the home team can be analyzed completely and studied repeatedly. Individual strengths and weaknesses are revealed. As a result, the errors of one's own team and players can be corrected and play improved. A plan of attack against the opponent can be determined.

Few schools will have sufficient funds to take pictures of all home games, but most can arrange for at least three. Eight hundred feet of film, at a total cost of approximately fifty dollars for sixteen-millimeter film, is adequate for a game. One can usually find someone in the community who is interested in and capable of taking the pictures, and most courts now have lights which are bright enough to produce clear pictures with the present equipment. For best results the pictures should be taken from as great a distance and as high above the floor as possible. It is better to locate the camera at a corner rather than in the center of the court, because this permits the lens to encompass the full court with little or no movement. By this procedure, all ten players can be held in view and their movement recorded. This is very important when pressing tactics and fast-break play are employed.

The pictures of a game can be shown to the squad, and they are available for the players to see individually in order to study their own characteristics of play. A coach may attempt to direct the action of a player on the court or to correct errors in technique without immediate success. He may call attention to errors of play in a game. The player may insist that he is not guilty of these errors, but when he sees them recorded on film, they stand out most glaringly. Usually correction takes place immediately.

On one occasion a coach thought a certain type of attack to be most effective in offsetting the defensive play of an opponent. The play was practiced repeatedly, but it did not seem possible for the players to put it into execution during a game although the opponent used the defensive pattern repeatedly. Finally, pictures were taken of a game with this team. When these were shown to the squad and the situation pointed out to them, the reaction was, "Oh, *that's* what you mean." In the very next game with this team, the defense was easily broken. The films accomplished what repeated explanations could not.

Coaching films are very useful if studied under guidance. There are many good films on the market which may be purchased or rented. The particular films one may use depend on the style of play and fundamentals which a coach is teaching. One should turn to the film indexes for information. Some manufacturers of athletic equipment have produced films that are obtainable on request, and some of these are very excellent for teaching purposes.

Loop films demonstrating fundamental techniques are excellent teaching devices. Their value is that they continuously repeat a desired technique so that each phase may be viewed in continuous succession until every detail is learned. Loop films are not used to the extent that their value justifies.

The author has found great value in making moving pictures of his own fundamental techniques and patterns of offensive and defensive play. These can be used most effectively in introducing the system of play to the new members of the squad each year and as a valuable review for the whole squad. Film used in this way can be a great time saver.

Thirty-five millimeter slides of successive positions and movements of fundamentals and play have value in the absence of motion pictures. When taken with a sequence camera, the shots need not be posed still pictures, but can be stages in actual court activity. Pictures of this type are sharper than the reproduction of frames from a motion picture film.

Sequence illustrations appear in sports magazines frequently. When these apply to the system of play or the fundamentals which a coach is teaching, he may post them on the bulletin board and call the attention of the squad to them. Again, some manufacturers of athletic equipment distribute these pictures as means of advertising, and enlarged copies of the illustrations are available.

USE OF STRATEGY BOARD

The strategy board has come into general use in coaching. It consists of a painted (usually green) metal surface on which a basketball court is laid out. Ten plastic blocks, five of one color and five of a contrasting color, which have magnets imbedded in them, represent the players. These may be placed on the board and moved about to show offensive and defensive patterns that a team plans to use, and to demonstrate set-ups to meet situations on offense or defense which may be presented by the opponent. These boards have an advantage over a blackboard in that the use of physical objects to represent players gives more reality and life to a presentation which on a blackboard is flat and consists of white lines and marks. The strategy board may be taken along on trips and used to set up play problems for the squad to solve, thereby stimulating thinking and concentration on basketball when there is usually nothing else to do. The players develop the habit of setting up problems for each other. In this way, the use of the board becomes an enjoyable game and, at the same time, provides an effective teaching situation.

The forerunner of the strategy board was the folded pasteboard court with ten checkers which "Red" Rolfe, the former Yankee third baseman, always carried in his coat pocket during the basketball season. "Red" was an ardent student and enthusiast of basketball. He coached basketball in New Hampshire during the winter while waiting for the next baseball season to roll around, and he never missed an opportunity to explore new ideas. At the time when the author's Stanford teams were electrifying Madison Square Garden fans with the innovation of the one-hand shot and a puzzling defensive system (the principles of which, incidentally, are now being adopted rather universally), "Red" was practically living with the Stanford squad, asking questions and demonstrating with his checker "strategy" board. He furnished good mental practice for the squad by stirring them to guide him through the intricacies of their defensive play on his checker board. This must have been the beginning of the modern-day strategy board.

RECORDING AND USE OF STATISTICS

Practice and game statistics are useful means of giving emphasis to the progress and needs of the players. The soundness, the aggressiveness, the carelessness, the accuracy, the alertness, and the qualities of team and individual play are reflected in the shooting record, the number of assists, the number of rebounds,

"Basketball Profile" Statistics Chart

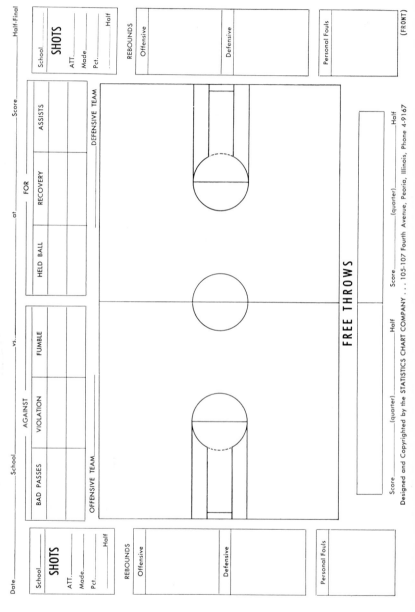

Date_____ School_____ vs._____ AGAINST_____ at_____ FOR_____ Score_____ Half-Final_____

SHOTS

School_____
ATT._____
Made._____
Pct._____ Half_____

REBOUNDS

Offensive

Defensive

Personal Fouls

DEFENSIVE TEAM

BAD PASSES	VIOLATION	FUMBLE	HELD BALL	RECOVERY	ASSISTS

OFFENSIVE TEAM

FREE THROWS

Score_____ (quarter). Half_____ Score_____ (quarter). Half_____

SHOTS

School_____
ATT._____
Made._____
Pct._____ Half_____

REBOUNDS

Offensive

Defensive

Personal Fouls

Designed and Copyrighted by the STATISTICS CHART COMPANY . . . 105-107 Fourth Avenue, Peoria, Illinois, Phone 4-9167

(FRONT)

126

"BASKETBALL PROFILE" STATISTICS CHART SUMMARY

DATE _____ TEAM _____ VS _____ AT _____ SCORE _____ OBSERVOR _____

NUMBER	NAME	SA	SM	PCT.	SA	SM	PCT.	OFF.	DEF.	P.F.	Bad Pass	Viol.	Fumb.	Held Ball	Recov.	Assists	Plus or Minus Points
PLAYERS		SHOTS			FREE THROWS			REBOUNDS			AGAINST			FOR			

TOTAL

SCHOOL _____

SCHOOL _____

(BACK)

127

the number of interceptions and recoveries, the number of fouls and violations, the bad passes, the held balls caused and permitted, and the offensive and defensive record. If these data are recorded, tabulated, and an accumulative game or practice record is posted for the players to study, this can have a very good motivating effect. The coach has a factual record to study and to aid him in the selection and handling of his squad. These data tend to correct or substantiate impressions of players and play formed during the course of a practice or a game. A single incident sometimes leads to an erroneous generalization about a player, whereas the factual record presents a more accurate picture.

One must remember that statistics do not give the total picture. Too much emphasis on statistics may create too much caution on the part of players with the result that their effectiveness is hindered. This can be damaging in cases where pressing, fast-break tactics form the basis of play. The author announced to his squad on one occasion that his selection of players for a Christmas trip would be based upon the accumulated statistical record which would be posted after each scrimmage. As the players weighed their chances by studying the record, they gradually developed a very conservative attitude in order to avoid mistakes that would affect their chances of making the trip. The coach was forced to abandon his extreme emphasis upon these statistics. It must be remembered that they are a helpful guide, but they do not tell the whole story about the players or the team.

Several managers who possess organization and concentration should be trained to take accurate, reliable records. They cannot be rooters or excited spectators; they must be detached from the game itself and completely impersonal to do an acceptable job.

Many forms have been devised for recording data. Coach Fordy Anderson developed a very satisfactory data sheet which may be purchased, the Profile Statistics Chart, on p. 126. The coach may desire to develop his own plan for recording practice and game results. The Individual Performance Chart, on p. 116, has been used for many years by the author. The data can be broken down so that the players can be compared in their various categories of play—best team players, best defensive players, best interceptors, best scorers, and so forth. They can also be rated on an all-round basis by adding the total record.

BULLETIN BOARDS AND MIMEOGRAPHED MATERIALS

The plan of reproducing play patterns, continuities, defensive formations and movements, instructions, and slogans so that the players have these to study and review can be very effective and speed up the perfection of play. Details and points of emphasis may be forgotten immediately after they are erased from the blackboard or spoken. The written record is there to refresh the memory. This material can be posted on the squad bulletin board or mimeographed and distributed to the squad. Some coaches are fearful lest this material fall into the hands of opponents. The fear is probably unjustified, because the players are just as eager as the coach to protect this information. Anyway, there are no secrets about sports; and, if it has taken hours of practice for your own team to perfect its play, an opponent will not have time to gain any more information than is available through scouting reports.

USE OF SCOUTING REPORTS

A digest of scouting reports, listing only the salient features which the coach feels should be brought to the attention of the squad, can be made before each game. This can consist of pertinent points on offense and defense which can be reviewed during the trip to a game away from home or passed from player to player the day of a game at home. These reports can include pithy phrases, humor, and slogans which can have a stimulating, high morale-producing effect. Once this practice is instituted, the players look forward to these reports with eagerness. A sample of such a report is shown below:

SCOUTING REPORT DIGEST

Piedmont vs. Visalia Aggies
	62		103

Personnel	*F.G.*	*F.T.*
5′ 11″ No. 3	— 4	— 3
5′ 11″ No. 11	— 9	— 2
6′ 6″ No. 13	— 19	— 7
6′ 4″ No. 15	— 8	— 2
6′ 4″ No. 41	— 7	— 4
6′ 4″ No. 43	— 4	— 1
	51	19

Digest of Piedmont Play

1. Piedmont badly outplayed by Aggies 103 to 62.
2. Aggies kept Piedmont off the boards and forced all shooting to outside.
3. Piedmont not a rugged team. Do not seem to like contact.
4. Did not show exceptional speed.
5. When Aggies ran, they dominated play.
6. Play man-to-man. Shift when screened. Sag to basket on a drive. Two-time ball at basket. Tie up rebounder.
7. On defense 13 is reluctant to follow away from basket. Stays back to get rebound.
8. Piedmont depends on 13. He always goes to his left. Uses jump shot entirely. Roves about the free-throw area.
9. Used back tip for control only.
10. Used box press with two front men two-timing during last of game.
11. Met Aggies at division line last five minutes of first half.
12. Forward and guard away from ball exchange.
13. Careless about keeping safety man back.
14. Use box on out-of-bounds.

Based on play against Aggies, we should:
1. Break on shot.

2. Half court press after three to five minutes.
3. Play in front of 13. Block out.
4. Shift on exchange away from ball.
5. Stay with guard on side with ball.
6. Use screens. Move the defense.
7. Play for steal on tip.
8. Drop off 13 when he gets ball at free throw with back to basket.

SQUAD LETTERS

The author has on occasion "published" a letter addressed to his squad as a means of building squad morale. It is surprising how much fun and interest can be developed in this manner. One must, of course, choose material which is adapted to his group and to the occasion. In all cases, the coach is working toward a specific objective. Spirit is by far the most potent factor in determining the outcome of sports contests; perfection of play without spirit or desire will not avail much, but spirit even in the absence of perfection of play can produce miracles.

TAPE RECORDINGS

Dictated recordings during the progress of a game provide a means of preserving impressions and observations of both player and team performance. It is helpful to analyze a game for the squad at its next meeting after the game. To do this one usually relies on his memory, but the memory is often faulty and can, as already noted, be warped by isolated events. Players often ask for advice concerning events that occur during the game. The coach may or may not recall accurately a particular situation. If, however, a dictaphone is placed at the bench, he may record his impressions and a running commentary on the game which will be very valuable to the players afterward when it is transcribed and placed at their disposal. This device has been used by some coaches with favorable results. The new portable dictaphones with rechargeable batteries make this coaching aid more practical than ever before.

OBSERVATION TOWER

Play can be observed and analyzed more clearly from a position close to but elevated above the court than from the level of the playing court. Scouts always prefer such a position to one at the press table next to the scorers. Many years ago Dr. Walter Meanwell did much of his coaching from a lookout spot above his practice court. He also preferred this spot during the progress of a scheduled game.

The author often takes a position on the motion picture platform above his court to conduct parts of his practice. He has sent players to this position to observe play so that they may get an over-all view of patterns of movement.

While at Springfield College, the author formed the habit of taking a position at the top of the bleachers in the field house to direct the movement of his team and to better observe the tactics of his opponents during the early moments of a game. In order to maintain contact with his assistant at the bench and the players during time-out, a two-way telephone system was installed. These tactics proved very helpful.

12

SCOUTING

Scouting is the art of observing, recording, and analyzing the play of an opponent for the purpose of determining the strategy and planning the type of team and individual play which is to be used against this opponent. Selected, pertinent information about an opponent, properly disseminated among the players, can save as much as ten minutes at the beginning of a game. This time is often spent in trial-and-error experimenting to find out the best tactics to use. If this can be determined before the contest and the players drilled in advance, a great advantage can be obtained. Players enter a game with greater confidence if they know what to expect from their opponents.

There are those who feel that time spent in scouting is wasted and that the information obtained is worthless. They claim that players are more often confused than helped by scouting information, and that teams never play the same anyway. So, if time is spent in preparation for a certain attack and something different is thrown at a team, the time is wasted and the team is completely demoralized. The best refutation of such an argument is the fact that players always play with greater surety and effectiveness when they meet a team the second time because of the familiarity attained from the first encounter. If this experience can be provided vicariously, a team need not sacrifice a first contest in preparation for subsequent meetings.

SCOUTING AGENCIES

Most coaches place great value on scouting, and they go to great expense to obtain advance information about their opponents. Because of this, several scouting agencies have been organized to provide coaches with information about teams. These agencies will provide reports on teams for fees varying from $15 to $50 plus expenses. These agencies are usually headed by former basketball players, coaches, or students of the game—people of considerable basketball experience. Their judgment is reliable, and they provide accurate and pertinent information. Of necessity, their service is impersonal, since they are not intimately acquainted with personnel of the team for which they are scouting. Their greatest value is that they can serve coaches who are unable, because of distance, to scout an opponent in person.

STAFF SCOUTING

As a rule, coaches prefer to do their own scouting or to have a member of their staff scout for them. Scouting information, to be of most value, must be related to one's own team; and only those who are familiar with the personnel of a team and its style of play are in a position to establish this relationship. Since the person who does the scouting is an authority on the game which he scouts, he is in the best position to evaluate the play of the opponent in terms of the team for which he is scouting. Hence, the desirability of using those who are intimately acquainted with the team for which the scouting report is made. Former players are often excellent scouts for their own team. They know the coach and his philosophy, and they know from having received scouting reports the kind of material that has value and the coach desires, and they can relate it to the team. Generally, fans and well-wishers, while well-meaning, have doubtful value as scouts.

The most valuable scouting record that one can compile is a report on all of his own games. To know the specific tactics an opponent uses against your team is worth more than the reports on all the other games played by this opponent. As a consequence, the author has always had his own games scouted, and he has kept a complete file of these reports. If a coach is at the same school for a number of years, these reports will reveal very clearly what to expect under given conditions. A study of these reports will reveal the strategy and philosophy of the coach as reflected by his team.

SCOUTING FORMS

For convenience in scouting games and as a means of reminding the scout of the various types of information desired, various types of scouting forms and check lists have been devised. There is no set pattern; therefore each coach may create his preferred design. The professional scouting services have their own forms.

One of the most complete and comprehensive published outlines has been devised by Howard Hobson,[1] whose team won the first official NCAA championship. While his form is rather cumbersome to use because of the dimensions of the document, it nevertheless provides for every type of information about an opponent.

The author has used a checklist together with blank forms for recording data about a team. He distributes these to his coaching classes as a guide in their scouting practice. This checklist and the accompanying forms are reproduced here for the attention of the reader.

Fordy Anderson, a former Stanford great, has devised one of the most compact scouting forms which has come to the attention of the author. It is shown on pp. 126-127.

---

[1] The All-American Basketball Player Record and Scout Book (New Haven: The Walker-Rockliff Company, n.d.).

SCOUTING PROCEDURE

The procedures for scouting a game, if one is to do an acceptable job, are really quite definite:

1. His preliminary preparation must be thorough. He should first be briefed on any specific information which is desired concerning the team to be scouted. He should study his checklist to refresh himself on the general scouting information for which he should be alert. He should check the time and place for the game, and make arrangements in advance for his scouting tickets. He should provide himself with all the work materials he may need such as notebook, shot charts, pencils, and clip board.

These points may seem to be trifling, but the neglect of any can materially handicap. For example, there are numerous instances when the time and place of a game have been changed so that the scout through neglect of this "minor" detail appeared at the wrong place for the game and so was unable to witness the contest.

BASKETBALL SCOUT REPORT

COLORADO STATE COLLEGE

SCOUT_____

On_____ vs._____ date_____ place_____

INSTRUCTIONS: (1) *Individual Shot Chart:* have someone keep this for you. Try to observe code for various types of shots. (2) *Team Offense and Defense Sheet:* follow instructions on sheet. (3) *Individual Techniques Sheet:* list player numbers in boxes. List name, height, weight, experience or class. Describe player strengths and weaknesses. Number Floor Plan to correspond with player number and diagram individual maneuvers. Use several Floor Plans if necessary to cover maneuvers of outstanding players. (4) Some items listed below might need amplification on an attached sheet. Use numbers of questions below where such amplification is indicated. If the question applies to individuals identify with player numbers only. Where indicated, underline identifying characteristics.

Team and Individual Characteristics—Offense

1. Is the team big   fast   smart   aggressive   in good condition?
2. Does the team have good competitive spirit? Yes   No.
3. Does the team show poise and confidence when in difficulty? Yes   No.
4. Do the men fight hard for rebounds?   Yes   No;   Numbers   .
5. Who gets good position for defensive rebounds?   Numbers   .
6. Who gets good position for offensive rebounds?   Numbers   .
7. Do they use a post attack?   Deep post?   Long post?   Double post?
8. How would you classify the post?   Shooter?   Screener? Feeder?   Clever?   Deceptive?
9. How do they feed the post?   From front?   From side? Off patterns?
10. Who feeds the post?   Numbers   .   Passes used? Direct?   Overhead?   Bounce?
11. Would you classify the team as being deliberate?   Patient? Hurried?
12. What players tend to make mistakes when under pressure? Numbers   .
13. What players show poise when under pressure? Numbers   .
14. What players are poor ball handlers?   Numbers   .
15. What players could be classed as good dribblers?   Numbers   .
16. What players could be classed as good drivers?   Numbers   .
17. What players are the best outshooters?   Numbers   .
18. What players "give and go" the best?   Numbers   .
19. What players use teammates for screens on two-man maneuvers?   Numbers   .
20. What two-man combinations work best for them?   Numbers   .
21. What players use "up-and-under" shots?   Numbers   .

22. What players could be classified as playmakers?   Numbers   .

Team and Individual Characteristics—Defense

23. How would you classify their defense?   Zone?   Man-for-man?   Combination?
24. Will the defense drop back when the ball is inside?   Yes   No   .
25. Do the individuals pick up for each other?   Yes   No   .
26. How will they defend a deep post?   High post?   Double post?   Diagram.
27. Will they use a press?   Yes   No;   Full court?   Three-quarter court?   Half court?
28. When will they press? Anytime?   When ahead?   When behind?   End of halves?
29. How would you classify their press?   Zone?   Man-for-man?   Combination?
30. Are they patient on defense?   Yes   No;   Players who are not patient?   Numbers   .
31. Will they switch on defense?   Yes   No;   In front?   In back?   Will post switch?   Yes   No   .
32. How will they play a driver?   Sag defense?   Turn outside?   Turn inside?
33. What players have fast hands in playing the ball?   Numbers   .
34. Will they pass ball back into lane after clearing board?   Numbers   .
35. Will they jump with jump-shooters?   Numbers   .
36. After clearing board where will outlet pass go?   Side?   Middle?   Short?   Long?
37. Diagram on separate sheet any peculiarities of free-throw line-up and jump balls.

2. The scout should be in his seat and ready to work well in advance of game time. He should secure a seat as high as possible in the stands near the center of the court so that his vision is unimpeded by spectators and so that he can get a clear view of the movements of all players at all times. A position at floor level is useless except for getting a close-up of players and comparing sizes at close range.

TEAM OFFENSE AND DEFENSE SHEET

OFFENSE: Number written description to correspond with diagram numbers. Show player numbers and position on floor. Do not forget out-of-bounds plays.
DEFENSE: Show by player number where player will likely cover and approximate depth from division line of front-line pickup. Describe defense and any peculiarities.

WRITTEN DESCRIPTION
OFFENSE

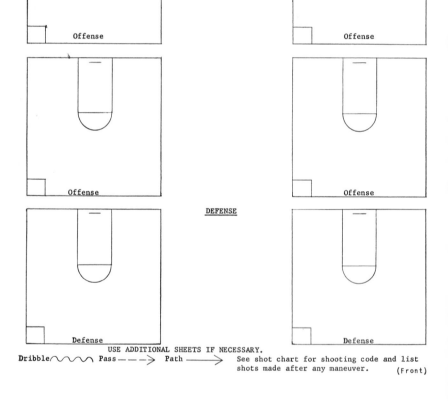

Offense

Offense

Offense

Offense

DEFENSE

Defense

Defense

USE ADDITIONAL SHEETS IF NECESSARY.

Dribble⌒⌒⌒ Pass — — —> Path ———> See shot chart for shooting code and list shots made after any maneuver. (Front)

140

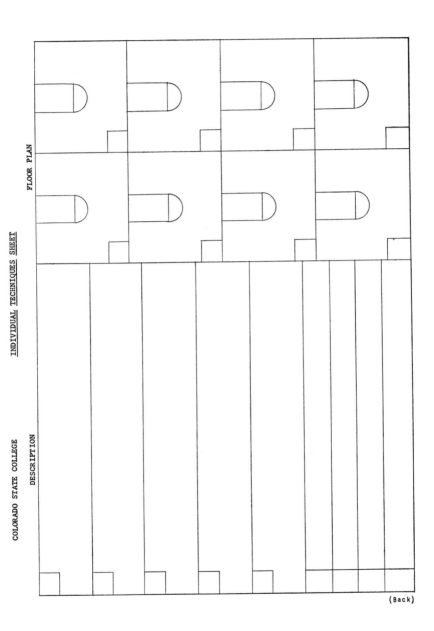

COLORADO STATE COLLEGE

INDIVIDUAL TECHNIQUES SHEET

FLOOR PLAN

DESCRIPTION

(Back)

141

_____ VS _____

AT _____ DATE _____

Encircle FG as: (J)

Code (if used): J–jump; L–LH Hook; R–RH Hook; 2–2 Hand set; 1–1 Hand set; D–Driving; T–Tip.

FGA____	FGA____	FGA____
No.____ FG____	No.____ FG____	No.____ FG____
Name_____ PCT____	Name_____ PCT____	Name_____ PCT____

FGA____	FGA____	FGA____
No.____ FG____	No.____ FG____	No.____ FG____
Name_____ PCT____	Name_____ PCT____	Name_____ PCT____

FGA____	FGA____	FGA____
No.____ FG____	No.____ FG____	No.____ FG____
Name_____ PCT____	Name_____ PCT____	Name_____ PCT____

TEAM TOTALS: FGA ____ FG ____ PCT ____ RECORDED BY _____

142

He should be in position soon enough to observe all of the preliminary work-out. Individual characteristics and play habits are by far the most important points of a scouting report. Often many of these characteristics are revealed during the warm-up period. Players almost invariably and intuitively practice the things they do best during the warm-up period. If they try other maneuvers at which they are not particularly adept, the contrast with their habitual actions is so striking that an astute scout is not misled.

The following true incident is related to indicate how valuable pre-game observations may be:

Coaching personnel had been changed at a certain school, and there was no opportunity to observe (to scout) the tactics which the new staff was teaching before a contest with his team. As a consequence, close watch was kept on the pre-game actions of his players.

It became apparent within a few moments after floor shooting practice began that this was a team of spot shooters, and that probably the pattern of play which the team would use was designed to accommodate each player in his favorite spot. Throughout the floor shooting practice, each player limited his shooting to a particular spot, and each was very accurate from that spot. There was one player who spent all his time feeding the others. He did not take a single shot at the basket throughout the floor warm-up. It seemed apparent that this boy was either a feeder or a bench warming sophomore.

This pattern of practice became so indelibly clear that the opposing coach (because he had no other information about this team) stopped the warm-up of his own team long enough to point out the spots from which each player shot. He instructed each to cover his opponent so closely that no unguarded shots would be permitted by these players from their favorite spots. He further advised to loosen the defense when a player left his spot. He also pointed out the player who never took a practice shot. He advised sagging off this player to help with the defense of the others. This was a calculated game risk which was to be followed until the opponents proved the pre-game analysis to be erroneous.

The analysis turned out to be absolutely accurate. The team was very mechanical and stereotyped in its play. The players were spot shooters, and were inaccurate when shooting from other positions. The boy who didn't take a practice shot started the game. He was the ball handler for the team, the feeder, and didn't take a single shot during the whole game. By adhering to the strategy devised on the spur of the moment, this team (composed of very talented players) was rather easily defeated.

3. The scout must adopt an impersonal and objective relationship toward the game. He must be coldly analytical. One cannot be a spectator or a rooter for a team or a player and do a reliable job of scouting. The moment personal feelings enter the picture, distorted observations and conclusions are likely to result. The effective scout is detached from his environment. He is intent upon observing every movement on the floor and from the bench, and he attempts to weave correctly all these actions into a logical whole. He can't do his job effectively if he permits himself to be distracted by his surroundings.

4. The scout should make as complete a recording as possible of the play throughout the game. Leaving points to memory and hoping to recall them later when the scouting report is being prepared is to take the chance of omitting important details or of introducing inaccurate statements. If all observations are in writing, even though specific facts may be repeated several times the total mass of material can be sifted later and the important points properly emphasized when the final report is being prepared.

5. Just what should be recorded when one is scouting a game? Certain things are routine. Shots and rebounds should always be recorded. If these are a part of the statistics kept and distributed by the host institution, then the scout is freer to concentrate on other details. If one is scouting alone and must record his own data, it is much simpler to keep a master shot chart for each player. An 8½" x 11" sheet of paper with the court marked off on it may be used for the purpose. The number of the player

placed on the location of the court from which the shot is taken is usually a sufficient record to keep. If the shot is made, a circle is drawn around the number. If one desires to indicate the kind of shot, he may use the legend indicated on check list shown on page 142. If a master shot chart is kept, it will be necessary to tabulate individual records after the game. Charts should be kept for both teams, and there should be a separate chart for each period.

It is sufficient merely to tabulate the rebounds for each player. This record should be kept for both teams and by periods. In order to keep accurate records, one must know what constitutes a shot and a rebound. The definition of a shot in the rule book does not include a tip. However, for statistical purposes, every attempt to score should be considered a shot. A rebound is credited to the person who first gains control of the ball after a missed shot. A controlled tip-out would constitute a rebound for the person tipping the ball.

One may check the accuracy of the recordings by checking the number of missed shots against the number of rebounds. Every missed shot must be offset by a rebound if the ball is alive after the miss. Shots that go out of bounds are recorded as team rebounds. Rebounds from missed free throws should be included in the record.

The height, weight, position, playing experience, and season record for each player should be secured. This information is usually available from the program.

The box score should be made a part of the record. It is not necessary to keep this as it can be obtained from the official scorebook after the game. Sometimes it is distributed by the publicity department at the end of each half.

During the warm-up period and as the game progresses, the pertinent characteristics of each player should be observed and recorded. These points include shooting and dribbling habits, passing ability, defensive strengths and weaknesses, quickness, condition, jumping ability, aggressiveness, and emotional control.

Some players seldom have any intention to shoot. Others will shoot if possible every time they get the ball. Some players hold the ball in one position to shoot and another to pass. Some must bounce the ball before they shoot. Some bounce the ball each time they receive it. Most players can dribble effectively with one hand only. Some are able to go only left or right when they dribble. Some players lack poise and are easily confused. They tend to fail when under extreme pressure. Some are dangerous ball stealers. Others are extremely clever and adept at getting good rebound positions. Left-handedness should be noted. When characteristics of this type tend to typify a player, they should be recorded.

All patterns of offensive and defensive movements with their attendant characteristics and effectiveness should be recorded. It is important to note position of players of both teams at the tip-off and during all jump balls as well as the direction of the tip and the movement of the players when the ball is tossed for the jump. The number of each player can be placed at the proper spot on the court.

The position of players at the beginning of an offensive movement should be noted. The general pattern of movement, if any, should be diagrammed. This may not be revealed at the onset; but as the game progresses and one continues to watch the play, the pattern will gradually become clear. Most teams use some definite pattern of movement, and scoring opportunities usually develop from this pattern. Therefore, if one is able to determine the general pattern, it will be easier to diagram the various plays which evolve from this pattern and it will be obvious how these fit into the general pattern of play.

Out-of-bounds formations and movements should be observed and recorded.

The line-up and tactics on free throws may prove to be important.

If a team employs a fast break, the pattern of movement and characteristics of the fast break should be diagrammed.

The general philosophy of the offense should be noted. Is the team conservative, does it work patiently for a particular shot or are shots made without hesitation whenever a player has an opportunity? Do the tactics of the team change at different stages of the game? What are the conditions under which changes take place? When time is taken out by a team, what change in tactics takes place when play is resumed? The scout should be alert for points of this kind.

What are the defensive characteristics of the team? The players' positions as they fall back on defense should be recorded; and if they are assigned to opponents, these assignments should be taken down. It should be noted whether or not there is any tendency to switch, and the conditions under which switching takes place.

If there does not seem to be any assignment to opponents, the movement of each player in the defense under given conditions and the general pattern of movement should be observed and recorded. It is not very revealing to indicate that a defense is man-to-man or zone of a certain type such as 2-1-2 or 3-2 or 1-3-1. This merely describes the initial formation or set-up. The movement of the players must be observed, recorded, and diagrammed to be useful in determining a method of attack to be used against the defense.

Some teams have chasers who go after the ball aggressively. Some defenses are designed to cover the player with the ball in a tenacious fashion and sag off of other players. Points of this kind should be carefully observed and recorded. Variation in tactics should also be observed.

Pressing tactics are being used more generally by teams. The pressing tactics and movements should be carefully analyzed or diagrammed. When they are used, it is of importance to observe whether the team members press full court, half court, keep pressure on the ball when it is in front of the defense, or use all of these tactics at various times. Does the team press only when it is desperate and at the end of a game, or are the tactics a fundamental part of its game? Are the tactics effective, and why?

The information on individuals and team play will accumulate as the game progresses. The same information may be recorded repeatedly as a running account is kept of the game. The fact that points are repeated gives strength to the pertinency of the point when later the scout is analyzing and sifting his notes in the preparation of his report.

While the scout is interested primarily in the team which he is scouting, he should not lose sight of the fact that the tactics of the opponents may in no small way be responsible for or *at least* influence the play of the team being scouted. As a consequence, a brief account of the play of the opponents with reference to its effect upon the team being scouted should be reported.

Of course, the score at various stages of the game may be of significance. There are those who believe that a report on the officials should also be included. The author does not, however, share this belief. It is seldom, if ever, that officiating or officials have any bearing on the outcome of a contest; because, after all, the work of the officials affects equally the play of both teams.

6. During time-out and at intermission, the scout should review his notes, record points that he has been carrying in his mind while play was in progress, and reflect on the play which has transpired up to the moment. He may even desire to make some analyses and summaries during the intermission. It is not desirable for him to spend his time in radio or television interviews or engaging in distracting sociability with spectators or friends. If he happens to have an assistant with him, they should discuss the play of the past period and get their plans organized for the next period. There may be points which will need to be checked during the second half as a result of a review of their notes.

One should not feel that he must be writing all the time. Often much more can be gained by merely sitting and intently observing the play until the pattern of attack and the strategy and reasons for it begin to reveal themselves. To see all the play and players, one should not focus attention on the ball as is the common habit of spectators. Rather, he should look ahead of the ball in order to see patterns and plays develop.

WRITING REPORT

The last job of the scout is to prepare his report. This should be done as soon as possible after the game—always before twenty-four hours elapse. The sooner one completes this job, the more accurate will be the report.

A well organized scouting report is divided into five parts—individual analysis and characteristics, offense, defense, summary, and recommendations. These parts should be submitted in this order. Information about the individuals is of greatest importance, and for this reason it is always listed at the beginning of the report.

1. All the pertinent facts about each player should be assembled from the notes. Those points which describe the outstanding characteristics of the player should be emphasized. They may represent strength or weakness. There may be one particular point of significance that is worthwhile passing on to the team, but only those characteristics which will be helpful in outplaying an opponent need be emphasized. A mere recitation of identifying characteristics will be of little value. Many times there is nothing of significance to report. The player is just a steady, run-of-the-mill player—neither outstandingly strong nor weak. When this is the conclusion it is helpful to say just that.

Players can be divided roughly into three groups—those who are outstanding or who have one or more very outstanding characteristics, those who are very poor players or have one or more very weak characteristics, and those who are run-of-the-mill players. Those in the last group are neither spectacular, nor are they inept performers. They are steady, dependable players whose play, for the most part, goes unnoticed. Those in the first two groups are always noticed either for their outstanding performance or for their very ineffective exhibition; but one may not be able to recall anything about those in the third group. This is a convenient rule-of-thumb method of grouping players.

The players should be listed in the order of their importance to their team in the game that was scouted. The most outstanding should be rated number one, the next number two, and so on. This procedure is helpful to the coach, because it focuses his attention on those players who may be expected to give the most trouble and who may need the most attention.

2. The offensive tactics are diagrammed and explained next. If one has a flexible defense (most teams have such defenses), it is possible to plan defensive maneuvers to interfere with the freedom of play of the opponents. It is difficult to alter offensive play effectively, because when habit patterns are formed, they are not easily changed. The offense of the opponent, therefore, is the second matter of importance to the coach.

First, the line-up and the movements at the tip-off at the beginning of the game should be diagrammed and explained; next, the position at which each player lines up to begin the offense and the general pattern of movement through the defense as well as the most frequently used and most effective scoring movement from this pattern should be considered in the same way. There may be only one or there may be several scoring movements. They should be presented in the order of their importance. If the team employs fast-break maneuvers, these should be diagrammed and explained. Then, jump-ball formations, out-of-bounds plays at each end and on the side, and offensive moves after a missed free throw should be shown. If the opponents use a pressing defense or any special type of defense, be sure to diagram and explain the offensive movement used against it.

Diagrams should be shown first and the explanation should follow immediately on the same page so that the two may be easily related. If an unorganized play of any kind is shown in any of the above aspects of offense, be sure to report this fact.

3. Next, the defense should be treated in much the same manner as the offense. First, the general type of defense used should be carefully diagrammed and explained. The position of

each player when the team drops back on defense should be shown. This is done by writing the number of the player in the proper position.

If the team is a pressing team, it is of particular importance to show and describe the formation and movement of this defense.

It is of very little help to report that a team plays a man-to-man defense, or that it plays a 2-1-2 or a 1-3-1 zone defense. In order to plan an offensive attack or to know what part of one's offense to concentrate against a particular team one must know detailed characteristics. Very few teams now employ a pure man-to-man or zone defense.

If the defense is in general a man-to-man type, one must know how closely each individual guards his man and how compact the defense forms about the goal; whether or not the players shift, and if they shift, whether or not it is only as a last resort; how far the players away from the ball sag from their opponents; if they have a tall player, whether or not he can be drawn away from the goal; whether or not a guard will follow his opponent away from the ball; whether or not a guard will leave his opponent to steal the ball; whether or not the defense watches the opponent to the exclusion of the ball; and how aggressive or conservative the defense is.

If the defense is in general a zone type of defense, it is important to know the general formation and position of players when they drop back on defense. In addition, one must know how compactly the defense is formed about the goal; how the defense moves as the ball and players penetrate it; what pattern of shifting is used; who covers the ball under specific situations; who the chasers are, and when they chase the ball. It is particularly important to recognize the tendency to overrush and the tendency to react to feigning movements.

The last two parts of the report tend to reveal the level of the discriminating judgment of the scout. These parts can be the most helpful to the coach.

4. In the summary, the scout digests the preceding three

parts. Here he should list only the salient features found in the body of the report. He is saying to the coach, "The preceding is a complete account of the game, but in my opinion, these are the features on which you should concentrate as you plan your game against this opponent. The complete report is presented for your information and study; however, if you take advantage of the points listed here in the summary, you'll be able to give the opponent the most trouble. I wouldn't worry too much about the rest of the report."

This summary should, of course, emphasize those points (individual characteristics, the offense, and the defense) which the scout thinks are of greatest importance and greatest value to the coach. Both strengths and weaknesses should be listed. There may be only three or four points; seldom will there be as many as ten.

5. The recommendations represent the judgment of the scout concerning the most effective methods to employ, in playing the opponent, against the points listed in the summary. For the scout to be able to recommend a method of attack and strategy of play, it is necessary for him to be familiar with the style of play of the team for which the report is prepared and he must know the philosophy of the coach. This emphasizes the reason, stated at the beginning, why the scout should be a member of the staff or closely associated with the team and coach.

The scout should have no hesitancy in presenting the materials suggested in the summary and recommendations. He is the authority concerning this particular game, and no other member of the team or staff has seen it. By this procedure, he gives the coach a graphic picture of the opponent and helps him to better visualize the type of play to be expected. The summary and recommendations are too often omitted from scouting reports. They are the most difficult to write. The foregoing, however, shows how valuable they are to the coach and how much is left to the imagination of the coach if they are omitted. The coach reserves the right to accept or reject any or all of these proposals.

He may make his own deductions if he chooses; but since he has not seen the game, an analysis by the scout as a result of a first-hand observation is much more helpful. That is why it is felt that to omit the last two parts of the report makes it incomplete, inconclusive, and weak.

A sample scouting report, in the format discussed above, follows. The names of the teams and the players are fictitious, but the report is of an actual game and is the exact report that was presented.

SCOUTING REPORT ON HAWAII COLLEGE

Alaska State vs. Hawaii College
February 26, 1960 at Honolulu

BY SAM JONES

SCORE: Alaska 83—Hawaii 77

Table of Contents

I. *General Statement*

This scouting report covers the Alaska State College–Hawaii College basketball game played at Honolulu Hall on February 26, 1960, in Honolulu, Hawaii. Alaska State won the game 83-77.

Hawaii College was a high-spirited ball club throughout the game and especially during the warm-up. They have a hustling ball club, and of the eight who played in this game, the majority were pretty fast and they handled the ball well.

The Hawaii College players are very ball-conscious, and whenever possible they will intercept passes.

Their offense is built around varied patterns from which they work for their jump shots. They took only two set shots during the entire game.

II. *Individual Report*

Number One—6′ 2″, 175-pound Jim Smith is our choice as the most important player for Hawaii College. Although Smith is only a sophomore, he played the whole game and picked up 23 points and 18 rebounds. He is a good jumper and has a good right-hand jump shot. Although not very large, Smith is a good rebounder and a good man to tip the ball back up. We rate Smith as a good, average ball player with good all-around abilities. His playing number is 31.

Number Two—Dave Peters is our next choice. He is an extremely fast man, good ball handler, and also one of their play makers. The 5′ 9″, 155-pound sophomore is a good defensive man because of his speed and good hands. He and Brown handled the ball well against the press and both seemed to possess good judgment. Peters had trouble hitting his right-hand jump shots both in warm-up and in the game. He started both halves and played a great deal of the ball game. He is an average ball player, but above average in speed. He got 5 points and 5 rebounds. Peters' playing number is 22.

Number Three—Jack Green is our third man. 6′ 6″, 205-pound Green works fairly well off his center position. He is a fair feeder and shoots a right-hand jump shot and hook shot pretty well. He started both halves and got 13 points and 13 rebounds while playing all but about three minutes of the game. Green is an average ball player and his playing number is 43.

Number Four—6′ 2″, 175-pound Don Warner is our choice for fourth position. Warner seemed to be one of few set shooters on the ball club. He shot set shots from the left-hand corner frequently during warm-up but shot only one long two-hand set during the game. He picked up 11 points and 10 rebounds while playing the better part of the game. Although Warner didn't start the second half, he came in to replace Miller who seemed to tire after playing a few minutes of the second half. Warner is right handed and possesses a good right-hand jump shot to go with his set shooting ability. His playing number is 32 and he is an average ball player.

Number Five—Dick Brown, a 5′ 11″, 170-pound junior is our fifth choice. Brown is a very good ball handler and can dribble with both hands. He brought the ball down the court on practically all their plays. He has a good right-handed jump shot that he was hitting from all over in warm-up, but he couldn't hit during the game. Although he got only 2 points and 3 rebounds, he is one of their play makers and started several plays from his guard position. His playing number is 21. Brown is an average ball player with an above-average jump shot.

Number Six—Our sixth choice, who showed very well when he played, is LeRoy Miller. Miller did not start, and he played very little of the first half. However, he did start the second half and picked up 14 points and 5 rebounds before being taken out before the midway point of the second half. He seemed tired when he was taken out. The 6′ 3″ senior has a good right-hand jump shot from the corner and around the upper part of the key. He is an average ball player and seemed to work in spurts. His number is 41.

Number Seven—Tony Martin, a junior guard, is our seventh choice. Martin is a good replacement for either Peters or Brown. He handles the ball well and jumps fairly well also. Martin didn't start either half but played enough to get 8 points and 1 rebound. Although he has a rather stocky build, he moves well and has good hands. His playing number is 33. He is an average ball player.

Number Eight—Art Johnson, a 6′ 4″, 215-pound junior is our last choice. Johnson, a replacement for Green, played very little of the ball game. He hooks and shoots jump shots with his right hand. He looked very unimpressive in warm-up. His playing number is 45.

The players listed below didn't play enough to affect the outcome:

No. 20 Bill McWilliams
No. 24 Jim Adams
No. 42 John Daniels
No. 44 Harry Davis

III. Offense

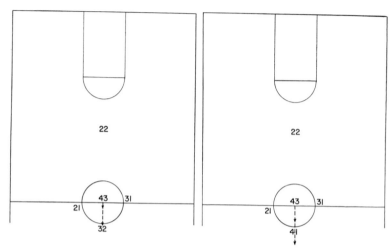

Center Jump Lineup, First Half. On the opening tip-off, the ball went to No. 32 for Hawaii College; but the team had not set up a definite play. Peters, No. 22, was deep safety man.

Center Jump Lineup, Second Half. Hawaii's line-up was the same as for the opening tip, except No. 41 replaced No. 32. However, Alaska tipped the ball to their deep man, No. 11.

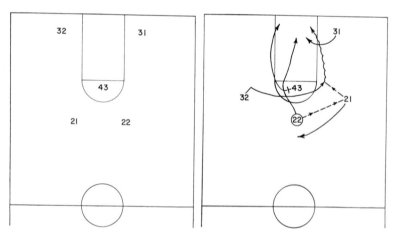

General Offense, 2-1-2. This was Hawaii's basic set-up, from which they ran several plays. It was their most effective basic pattern. On following pages are other common variations.

1-3-1 Offense. Used by Hawaii on four or five plays, and on two of them they scored easy layups. At the other times, side men worked for open jump shots before definite plays developed.

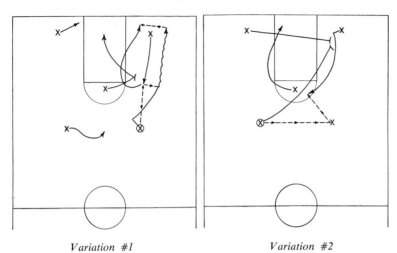

Variation #1   *Variation #2*

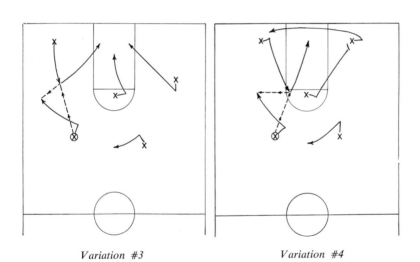

Variation #3   *Variation #4*

III. *Offense* (Cont.)

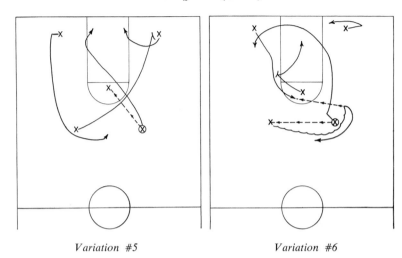

Variation #5　　　　　　　*Variation #6*

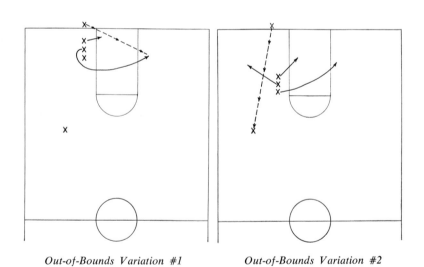

Out-of-Bounds Variation #1　　　*Out-of-Bounds Variation #2*

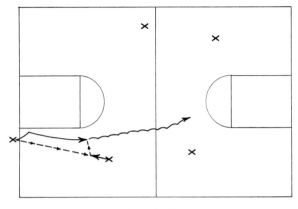

Against the Press

IV. *Defense*

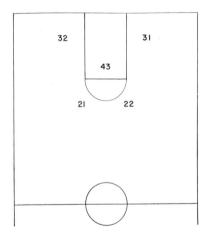

Hawaii College used two different defenses during the game. Their most popular defense was the straight man-to-man. They did switch when they ran into a screen.

Their second defense was a 2-1-2 zone. They covered anyone who came into their assigned area. They had no set assignments as far as men go.

INDIVIDUAL SHOT CHART
Hawaii College

No.	FGA	FGM	FTA	FTM
22	13	2	2	1
21	11	1	0	0
31	21	8	11	7
32	13	5	4	1
33	8	3	3	2
43	17	4	7	5
45	1	0	2	1
41	10	6	3	2
Total	94	29	32	19

Alaska State College

No.	FGA	FGM	FTA	FTM
4	10	3	0	0
5	8	4	5	3
11	14	7	1	0
21	24	9	7	5
32	21	6	5	5
31	2	0	0	0
23	14	6	2	0
14	0	0	1	0
Total	93	35	21	13

REBOUNDS
Hawaii College

No.	Offensive	Defensive	Total
21	1	2	3
22	3	2	5
31	11	7	18
32	3	7	10
33	1	0	1
41	1	4	5
45	1	1	2
43	9	4	13
Team	8	3	11
Totals	38	30	68

Alaska State College

No.	Offensive	Defensive	Total
23	5	7	12
4	5	1	6
21	8	11	19
5	5	5	10
31	2	0	2
11	1	2	3
32	1	2	3
Team	9	2	11
Totals	36	30	66

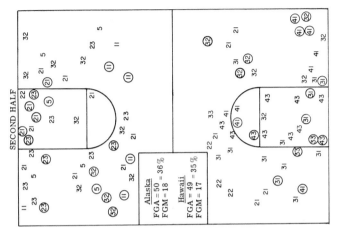

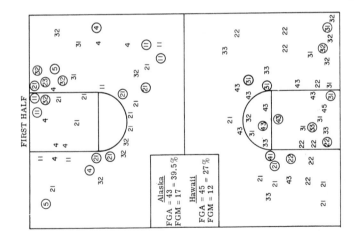

FIRST HALF

Alaska
FGA = 43 = 39.5%
FGM = 17

Hawaii
FGA = 45 = 27%
FGM = 12

SECOND HALF

Alaska
FGA = 50 = 36%
FGM = 18

Hawaii
FGA = 49 = 35%
FGM = 17

GAME STATISTICS

Alaska   FGA = 93 = 38%   FTA = 21 = 62%
          FGM = 35   FTM = 13

Hawaii   FGA = 94 = 31%   FTA = 32 = 59%
          FGM = 29   FTM = 19

161

They picked up Alaska State as they crossed the center line. They kept two men back as safeties on all free throws that they attempted. They also had two safety men on all jump balls. They played an aggressive defense, taking chances on intercepting passes from guards to forwards.

V. *Summary*

1. Hawaii College has a multitude of plays that they move their offense on.
2. Their team is fast, and the team as a whole handles the ball well.
3. They have a good rebounder and all-around ability man in No. 31, Smith.
4. Hawaii College broke up a full-court press by using their two guards to dribble the ball down while the other three men took their defensive men to the sidelines in order to give the guards room to work.
5. No. 41, Miller, although he played only briefly, showed a very accurate jump shot from all over the court by hitting six for ten from the field.
6. Their offense is built around jump shots. Only two set shots were taken the whole game.
7. Hawaii College moved from a man-to-man defense to a 2-1-2 zone at the command of one of the guards.
8. Hawaii College made a number of interceptions on passes that went from guard to forward.

VI. *Recommendations*

1. Keep No. 31, Smith, away from the boards.
2. Don't let Miller jump if he is hitting.
3. If you press them, get on the man who takes the toss-in as quickly as possible.
4. When on defense, don't stick to the front men too closely; Hawaii College doesn't shoot set shots but drives or cuts around the front defensive men for jump shots.
5. Uses bounce passes to cut down on interceptions.

13

STRATEGIC
SITUATIONS

There are three general rules which should guide one in his plans for meeting an opponent.

1. Don't play your opponent's type of game unless that is your best game.
2. Make your opponent play your style of game.
3. Be prepared for any eventuality.

While the meanings of these three statements are more or less self-evident, a few explanatory statements may help to implement them in basketball situations. If the opponent can control the general pattern and tempo of play, he should have an advantage. This is particularly true if the play of the opponent is contrary to that preferred by one's own team. For example, if the opponent is drilled in a ball-control type of game while one's own team is conditioned for a fast-break game, the opponent will have a decided advantage if he can control the tempo of play. Slow-down tactics will tend to frustrate the team that prefers the fast break. The players become impatient; they get erratic and hurried when they get the ball. Finally, they are lulled unconsciously into the same tempo. As a result, they do not perform as capably as usual.

Several years ago the University of Kentucky and the University of Utah met in the finals of a national tournament. Utah realized it could not match strides with the speedy Kentucky team. As a consequence, it determined upon slow-down tactics. When the ball was recovered from the Kentucky backboard, no effort was made to fast-break. The player with the ball would wait until the opponents dropped back on defense. Then one player, a clever, dependable boy with the ball, would dribble the ball no faster than a walk to the front court. Once in the front court, the ball was carefully and slowly nursed to an open spot before a shot was taken. The Kentucky team did not seem to be able to change the tempo of play. As a consequence, these tactics worked so successfully that Utah won the game.

On another occasion the University of Colorado was playing San Francisco University in the semi-finals of the National Collegiate Tournament. San Francisco University had the great rebounding and defensive star, Russell. Coach H. B. Lee of Colorado knew that his team was no match for the San Francisco University champion if he traded shots with it. He was sure that the chances of his team's regaining the ball after a missed shot were practically nil. Further, he knew that to attempt to get a close-in shot over Russell would be wishful thinking. Therefore, he chose to control the ball until good, unhurried shots were obtained. Although his team did not win the game, it played one of the best and most exciting games in national tournament play; and his team was in striking distance of victory throughout the contest. Had his star player not been lost before the game as a result of a badly sprained ankle during the preliminary game practice, who knows but that the results may have been different.

On another occasion, Kansas and the University of North Carolina were locked in the finals of the NCAA Tournament. The circumstances were similar to the Colorado-S.F.U. contest. The great Chamberlain was playing for Kansas. North Carolina elected to control the ball in order to force Chamberlain away from the goal. These tactics were successful. The score was very close at all times. It went into three overtime periods. North Carolina finally emerged the victor. It is the consensus that, had North Carolina resorted to the Kansas style of play, the contest would have ended in a rout for Kansas.

There are times, of course, when the play of the opponent is also the strongest type of game that one's own team plays. If it is the judgment of the coach that for the best results he should stick to his own pattern of play in spite of this fact, then, of course, that is the best strategy. Invariably, a team will do its best while playing the style of game to which it is accustomed. It is not an easy matter to change the habits of players.

These examples support the first two rules for determining the strategy of play that one should employ against an opponent. Rule three, "Be prepared for any eventuality," has many coaching implications. It suggests practice programs. The game of basketball as played by high schools and colleges has so many variations and types of offense and defense that one must be prepared to combat a wide range of tactics. The ingenuity and imagination of coaches know no bounds; and this is why high school and college basketball is so interesting and exciting. There is no monotonous sameness of play, and almost anything may happen. The rules committee has wisely permitted, even encouraged, originality and variation. It has refused to legislate the style of play which a coach must employ, and thus, the committee does not inhibit him in his efforts to offset inequalities in personnel by thwarting him in his range of strategy. A coach who does not anticipate game situations that may arise and prepare his team for them in his general program of practice is likely to regret this neglect at an important time in the season.

A case in point was brought to light in a recent national tournament. One of the teams engaged in the finals was one of the foremost pressing teams in the country. Evidently it spent much time in practice on pressing tactics. It must, however, have given only lip service to defense against the press. As a consequence, when it met a team which pressed equally well, it was unprepared. Its play became erratic, there was much confusion, many bad passes were made, and interceptions were numerous. As a consequence, it was nosed out by an opponent which had not been conceded much of a chance.

Generally speaking, teams seem to panic more when playing against zone defenses. This is usually because they are not prepared to combat adequately this style of defensive play. A team whose style of play is designed to work as effectively against one defense as another is, of course, the best prepared.

A team which does not practice against a fast break is likely to be in trouble when it competes against this method of play. Further, a team which never practices a fast break itself will be decidedly handicapped if on some occasion its opponent forces it into race-horse basketball. Incidentally, it is much more difficult to play this style of game than the methodical ball-control game. Ball handling is much more difficult, and there is a greater tendency to be tricked into this style of play. Once the race-horsing starts, it is hard to stop. It is like a forest fire before a strong wind. A team that is not prepared to shift or switch may meet a team that uses effective screens, making shifting absolutely necessary. When this occasion arises, the unprepared team will be in trouble and may lose because of this one fact.

Teams which over-sag toward the ball and have not practiced close guarding tactics may fall prey to unorthodox cross-court passes. This situation occurred in a recent national tournament. Since this type of pass was used throughout the game and was never once intercepted, it became evident that the tactic of "over sagging" was so imbedded in the habits of the players that they could not meet even an unorthodox situation.

These examples may be multiplied. They will suffice to indicate the necessity of being prepared for any eventuality.

In addition to the general rules for strategy, there are many specific rules which are generally accepted practice. Several are listed in the next chapter as a guide to the young coach who may at some time be faced with the problem of meeting teams where some or all of these guides will be useful.

14

COACHING STRATEGY

Coaches are constantly required to make decisions quickly during the course of a game. The plan of play has usually been worked out in advance; but, often, conditions change and altered plans are necessary. The success with which these changes are made may mean the difference between victory and defeat.

When and how should time-outs be used? When and for what reasons should one substitute? When and under what conditions should a pressing defensive be used? When should a team freeze the ball? When is the fast break indicated? When should ball control be employed? When should offensive and defensive tactics be changed?

Each game and each situation has varying factors so that it is not possible to cover every one in a specific manner. If this were possible, most of the thrill and chance would be taken out of the game for both the coach and the players. Also, different coaches may analyze and react to a given situation in a different manner. The philosophy and background of the coach will partly determine his moves. Also, the preparation of his squad and the available personnel are conditioning factors.

There are, however, general guides which may be helpful. These will be presented. Actual examples will be given to show the implementation of these guides.

An over-all guide for governing play against an opponent is to employ those tactics which are most aggravating and frustrating. Another way to state this principle is, "Play the way your opponent does not want you to play." In order to be able to implement such a principle, it is necessary to have a team and its players trained in versatility. Unless one prepares his team and players in practice to execute many types of tactics, it is asking too much to expect them to employ new tactics on the basis of directions given during the progress of a game. Even though the tactics may not represent the type of game one plays best, they will nevertheless be profitable if they tend to disorganize and disarm an opponent.

Strategy of this kind presupposes an accurate knowledge of the opponent as well as of the philosophy of the coach. Thorough scouting reports provide the former; and a knowledge of the background of the coach and the observation of his methods over a period of time provide the latter. With this information, a period of several days prior to a contest may be spent in rehearsing the tactics to be used against an opponent. Most teams adopt a definite pattern of play from which they cannot deviate with success. For this reason, preparation of this kind can be carried out to great advantage.

STRATEGY FOR THE INDIVIDUAL

The following are examples of strategy which show how this philosophy of play has paid dividends by turning possible, even sure, defeat into victory. Each represents an actual case, but games and teams are not identified in order to avoid the appearance of criticism of a coach or the embarrassment of a player. Most are from recent games.

1. In a recent NCAA play-off game, the star of one team seemed to score at will; and this team left the floor at half-time with a comfortable lead. This occurred despite the fact that the team had been scouted, the tactics of this player had been thoroughly analyzed, and a plan had been devised and practiced

for stopping him. He had developed the habit of faking in one direction and then moving in the opposite before going up for a jump shot with which he was deadly accurate. The star was so quick and effective with these tactics that opponents were afraid not to move with his fake for fear he might move in the direction of the fake. This was true of the player in this game who was assigned to stop the star during the first half. But during the second half, the guard made the correct moves and stopped the star without a field goal. Not only that, but he stole the ball from him several times, completely upset the poise of this star player, and caused him to press so badly that he became a detriment to his team and had to be removed from the game. Needless to say, the team that had been in the lead at the half lost the game in the last minute of play. Here is the case of a player who was stereotyped in his habits of play and an opponent who did what this player did not want him to do. The outcome of a game hinged upon this kind of strategy.

2. A similar situation is the case of a star player who was averaging close to thirty points per game. The team of this player usually was sparked by its star. One opponent decided to concentrate on this one player at the risk of letting others on the team be unguarded. The concentration on the star held him to three field goals and permitted a team that would have been beaten with comparative ease to win by more than twenty points.

3. In another NCAA tournament game an offensive star who was a weak defensive player was continually maneuvered into a position where he was forced to cover a player driving for the goal. In a short while, he had been charged with four personal fouls. As a result, he was forced to let offensive players dribble to the goal unguarded for fear he would commit his fifth foul and thus be lost to his team for his offensive value for all the game remaining. Here is a case of capitalizing on a known defensive weakness of a star scorer.

4. A star of some years past was a terrific dribbler with driving speed that prevented most opponents from guarding or stop-

ping him. It was observed, however, that he had developed the habit of dribbling only to the outside. A guard was instructed to overplay to the outside until this player demonstrated that he could dribble successfully to the inside. The result was that the effectiveness of this player was completely erased. He tried to move inside but without success. Completely unorthodox defensive tactics were employed but they accomplished the purpose. The player was prevented from doing what he wanted to do. He was so conditioned to a single maneuver that he was unable to change.

These are examples of employing the principle of "preventing a player from doing what he wants to do." These examples can be multiplied without end but are undoubtedly sufficient to indicate the possibilities and to stimulate one's imagination so that he can make adaptations and devise strategies in other or similar situations.

TEAM STRATEGY

The following are a few examples of the application of the same principle in situations of team play that may be helpful to the reader.

1. One of the top teams in the country was stopped by a relatively weak team. This was done by tactics designed to offset the strength of the opponents, who had built all of their offense about their top-ranking center. This team had been so successful in its single-post attack that it had not found it necessary to resort to another type of play. Its attack always started after the ball was fed to the post; and gambling on this bit of observation, the weak team played to prevent the ball from getting to the post by playing in front of the post and sagging another defensive player to a spot behind the post. This trick so surprised and frustrated its opponent that the weaker team was victorious by a margin of a single point whereas previously it had been beaten by twenty points. The amazing part of the play was the fact that the single-post team continued to try to force the ball

to the post throughout the game only to have it intercepted time after time. Evidently this team became so conditioned to this one pattern of play that when an effective defense was set against it, either it could not believe it was stopped or it was unable to change its tactics. This, of course, reveals weakness in a team which lacks flexibility in its attack. Most teams, however, at some time fall prey to inflexibility.

2. On another occasion a team with four players over 6'6" had designed its attack so that no shots were taken except close-in shots developed from a double-post offense. This planning was meant, of course, to utilize the dominating height of its four big players. A small team (with only one player as tall as 6'3"), in addition to running this big team, employed a defense that always placed a player in front of and behind each big man at the basket. The defense would drop off the man with the ball on the side or in front and give this man a free shot rather than permit the ball to be passed into the basket. Surprisingly, this big team refused the outside shots and continued to try to work the ball in closer to the basket. They were beaten by twelve points. Toward the end of the game, they tried outside shots but they were so conditioned to their other type of play that, although the players were in advantageous positions, there was no confidence in outside shooting and thus no effectiveness.

3. In a quarter-final NCAA game some years ago, a team was known to use the usual attack against a zone defense—to stand still and try to out-pass the defense. A team which was not particularly adept at playing a zone started the game with its customary man-to-man play but soon found itself unable to cope with the driving offensive play of its faster opponent. It went into a zone which immediately caused its opponent to change its offensive tactics to a standstill pass pattern. As soon as this occurred, its opponent went back to its man-to-man play but this was never discovered because of the standstill tactics. As a result, the game became a close contest and, although the weaker opponent did not win, it had the opportunity and lost by only a very small margin.

4. A team with a versatile attack in which any player could play in any position was playing a team which had a tremendous rebounder of 6′9″ and a speedy, clever "ball hawk." This team was winning its games by the use of a lightning-like fast break started by its great boardman and by interceptions from the clever work of its "ball hawk." The team was using a man-to-man defense. To offset this advantage, its opponent revolved its offense until the rebounder was playing out in front and the "ball hawk" was in the rebounding position. This stopped the fast break, prevented interceptions, and made an even game out of what otherwise would have been a walkaway.

5. Many teams resort to ball-control tactics. Such teams seldom, if ever, use the fast break. They prefer to maneuver the ball until their opponent makes a mistake on which they can capitalize. Every move of such a team is made according to pattern. If permitted to play its own game, such a team will look great. Its play will be as smooth and regular as the movement of a clock. It will hold down the score and spectators are likely to comment erroneously on the great defensive strength of this team. If, however, it is not given time or opportunity to set its own pace and pattern, it will usually fall apart. It is so much easier to play slowly and deliberately than to play fast and aggressively; moreover the deliberate team is unable to adjust to the faster tempo of play, and it becomes erratic.

The most striking example of the efficiency of this kind of strategy was an NCAA final. A perfect ball-control team was ignominiously defeated when its opponent resorted to forcing tactics and to a fast break.

6. One year, a National Invitational Tournament final was won by the reverse tactics. A normally fast-breaking team realized that it was no match if it played its opponent's game. It had one very good ball handler so it got the ball to him after every exchange of control and he literally slowed the game down to a walk. He would actually walk as he dribbled from the back court to the front court. No shots were taken until the ball was worked in for a comparatively close-in shot. As a result of this

strategy, it was able to keep pace with its bigger and faster opponent and won the game at the end.

These last two examples not only illustrate the validity of the philosophy of not permitting a team to play the way it wants to play but also the advantage to the team that is able to dictate the pattern and tempo of the play.

7. A ball-control team is seldom as well conditioned as a pressing, fast-breaking team. So, in addition to upsetting the poise of such a team by forcing it to play a type of game it does not want to play, it is possible to run the ball-control team down before the end of the contest. The results may not show until late in the second half, but in the end the difference in condition becomes evident and it is surprising how a large divergence in the scores can be erased in a very few minutes. The opponent becomes not only tired but also erratic.

The writer has had several experiences that demonstrate the effectiveness of this type of strategy. There were two opponents, one on the East Coast and one on the West, which seldom, if ever, won a game against this type of strategy in spite of their superior talent. Year after year and game after game these opponents would have what might appear to be a commanding lead at the end of the first half only to lose, sometimes by a wide margin, at the end. The advantage of fast play, fast break, and full-court pressing is that the opponent cannot avoid playing a fast, hurried game. If he is not in condition and is not trained to play fast, eventually he always suffers as a result of fatigue which causes erratic play and ineffective shooting.

On another occasion a team that was pressing and fast-breaking was behind throughout the game (as much as twenty-four points in the second half, and eleven points when there were just a few seconds more than two minutes to play); yet it won the game with a shot that went through the basket as time expired. Old man fatigue was finally a factor and spoiled an opportunity for great jubilation by the tiring opponent.

8. A change of tactics on the spur of the moment to counteract a move by an opponent or to meet a situation that arises sud-

denly during a contest requires that the coach follow the moves of his opponent attentively at all times. Three illustrations of game situations will illustrate this point:

(a) In a two-game series it was found that the pivot could operate at will. All play was directed to him in the first game and, as a consequence, he was able to score over thirty points. In the second game, the opposing coach strengthened his defense at this position by dropping off of the ball at the side to prevent a pass to the center. The side man was not a scoring threat but a strong rebound player and fast.

To thwart this bit of strategy by the opponent, a player who was an excellent shot but very slow was substituted for the side man with instructions to shoot every time he got the ball until his opponent came out on him so that he could pass to his pivot. The defense continued to sag so that the substitute scored four times in succession. This was sufficient to open up the pivot again so play could proceed as in the first game.

(b) In another game the pivot man had carried the burden of scoring. He was very accurate in this particular game so the team was instructed to capitalize on his scoring by getting the ball to him whenever possible. The game was a see-saw affair; and with forty-five seconds to play the score was tied, largely through the efforts of this pivot man.

Time was taken out with the ball in control of his team. It was reasoned that since the pivot had been the effective scoring threat throughout the game the opponents would logically conclude that the ball would be passed to him for the last shot. Consequently, the play was set to pass to the pivot in order to concentrate the defense on him and then to have him pass off to another player for the final shot.

The ball was controlled until the last few seconds

when this strategy was executed. It worked as planned so that the player who made the final shot had an unhurried opportunity. He scored and the game ended as the ball went through the basket.

(c) Scouting reports indicated that a team had strong outside shots but that they needed plenty of time to make their shots. When this point was further proved during the progress of a game, the defense was changed suddenly from a massed defense around the goal to a pressing defense. The outside players not only were stopped from scoring but also they became hurried and erratic in their play. The tide of the game was completely changed from an even contest to a rout.

SUMMARY OF STRATEGY

The foregoing examples of actual play situations may be summarized to cover strategy in general as follows:

1. Force your opponent to do the things he does not want to do. Players and coaches often become confused and even panicky when their normal pattern of play is blocked.

2. Try to set the pattern of play by forcing your opponent to play your game. Outstanding teams can be tricked into this kind of play.

3. Substitute only for tactical purposes. A particular game situation requires a player with a special talent. A good shooter is needed at a particular moment. A strong defensive player is needed to stop a star. Rebound strength is needed. A regular in a particular game may not be playing his usually strong game so that his substitute is better at winning. A whole team may be "off" so that all efforts to get them to play have failed. The substitution of a whole new team is indicated.

It is seldom wise to remove a player for making a mistake. To substitute under such circumstances will tend to destroy confidence, and it may destroy the effectiveness of a conscientious player for the rest of the season.

4. Take time out for tactical reasons only. Time-outs for injuries are not included here because these can be cancelled by substitutions. But if an opponent scores three times in succession without a counter score, it is wise to call a time-out in order to analyze the situation and make changes in play as may be indicated. The brief interruption of the game often stops the scoring spree.

If a team becomes erratic or disorganized, time should be called in order to recoup and to get play reorganized. A complete change of tactics may be indicated.

In a particularly evenly contested game, if a weakness is discovered in the opponent's play, a time-out to plan to take advantage of the weakness may change the whole complexion of the game.

In the second half, as the game reaches its crucial stages, it is wise to call a time-out to make plans and to make sure that all players understand the strategy to be employed.

So far as possible, a team should save its time-outs for the second half.

Time-out should never be taken to rest.

Time-out should never be requested by the team that is dominating the play or that is in a scoring spree. Let the opponent use his time-outs in these cases.

5. Pressing tactics have value in many situations and can be employed effectively at many stages of a game; but there is no fixed rule to determine when to use them. The fact that a team is a dangerous pressing team often is sufficient; and though the press may not be used, the fact that an opponent is expecting it at any moment can have a demoralizing psychological effect.

Pressing is always effective against a slow or inexperienced team. It can be used against such teams at any time and until complete mastery of the game is obtained. Against a strong team, varied tactics should be employed. In any case, it is usually more effective to alternate pressing and regular play, to alternate full-court and half-court press. This prevents a seasoned team from adjusting to the defense readily. Giving this team a steady diet of pressing will permit it to organize effectively to meet it. If the press has been used effectively against such a team and it takes time-outs to organize, it is good strategy to call off the press for a few minutes and then re-employ it. By such tactics, the value of the opponent's time-out to reorganize is often lost.

The press is effective merely to change the tempo of the game and to disrupt the planned play of a team. In this respect it can be used at the beginning of and toward the end of the first half, at the beginning of the second half, and in the early minutes of the last quarter of a game. One should never wait until the last few minutes to employ the press, became it takes time for the results of a press to show. Therefore, using it in the last moments of a game usually amounts to desperation tactics, the admission of defeat, a so-what attitude: "We are beaten so we may as well try the press." If the press has value, it should be used in a positive way. It has no value as a lost cause. The psychological effect of the press on the players is demoralizing when thought of in this fashion.

The press has value to get one's own team moving on nights when both the offense and the defense are lagging. Moreover, to encourage individual initiative, surprise pressing tactics are excellent strategy and take advantage of a team that has been lulled into a state of complacency to the extent that it becomes callous and inattentive in handling the ball in the back court and in the front court in front of the defense. These tactics are best used after a team has been conditioned to a retreating or passive defense.

6. Much of what has been written about the use of the press may be said of the fast break. A team may use the fast break as a basis of its offensive play or it may use it whenever the opportunity presents itself. The mere threat of a fast break is often a sufficient deterrent to cause an opponent to play cautious and conservative offense. A championship was won in this way, when a coach was so fearful of the fast break of his opponent that he permitted only one man to rebound after a shot. The others

dropped back on defense immediately after a shot. The opponent, of course, had little opportunity to fast-break but the threat of its lightning-like fast break was just as effective.

7. Ball-control tactics have a definite place in basketball. When a team is badly outmanned with respect to size, its only hope after the defense is set is to control the ball until it can secure a good, unhurried shot. Its chances of securing the rebound, if the shot is missed, are very limited. It is good judgment, therefore, for this team to control the ball until it can get a shot at a position from which its chances of scoring are as great as possible.

The employment of ball control under these circumstances is legitimate because the team is positive in its efforts. It is working to get a good shot, not necessarily a lay-up. It is not holding the ball and refusing to shoot to hold the score down. Such tactics are never to be condoned. They represent a defeatist attitude that is not good for the players and is certainly not good for the game. It makes a farce of it. A coach who would teach this type of play is a detriment to the game, and he should be severely censured.

Ball control employed strategically as indicated is a definite part of basketball. It is one of the main reasons why a time limit should never be introduced into the amateur game. It may be used effectively, also, to help a team smooth out its play. When a team becomes sloppy, erratic, and uncoordinated it can recover its smoothness and coordinate its movement by a short period of passing within its pattern before attempting a shot. Teams which employ a continuity of movement find this tactic very helpful.

8. Freezing tactics—controlling the ball when the team is ahead but there is no intention of taking a shot—should never be employed. Usually used toward the end of the game, their purpose is to pull the defense out and away from the basket.

Such tactics usually destroy the offensive effectiveness of a team and give it a negative attitude. To use such tactics when a team is scoring and has built up a lead usually puts it back on its heels and causes it to lose its scoring touch.

There should always be the aim to score and to keep the team offensive minded. When a team is ahead at the end of the game, it should work for a lay-up shot only. At the other stages in the game, it should work for either lay-up shots or shots when the shooter is poised, balanced, and unhurried. But, always, there should be the objective to score.

9. Defensively, it is good judgment to mass the defense about the goal against a team that has no shooting strength outside but handles the ball well and has good inside shots. The same strategy should be used to stop inside strength under any circumstances.

10. Always plan defense in order to stop the offensive strength of the opponent, even at the expense of weakening the defense at other spots. Some coaches reason that one must concede the star his points and stop others. This hardly seems logical in view of the fact that a team invariably looks to its strength for its inspiration. If this is stopped, the chances for victory would seem to be much enhanced. One of the examples given earlier was in line with this type of thinking.

11. Offensively a team should direct its attack at the weakness of its opponent's defense. This weakness, if it exists, may be in an individual or it may be in the pattern of the defense itself. One of the examples of an NCAA game related earlier demonstrated how one team employed this tactic.

15

PRE-GAME PREPARATION

Pre-game preparation begins on the afternoon of the day of the game, and it has to do with mental and emotional, as well as physical, preparation. Since conditions are quite different, the plans for home and away games are different. At home, one is in his normal environment: therefore, from the standpoint of emotional preparation, it is better to permit the players to continue their normal pursuits. In the interest of the conservation of energy, the normal program is sometimes partially altered. For example, arrangements may be made for the players to rest in the afternoon before the game.

When the team is traveling, conditions are decidedly unnatural. Boys are thrown out of their routines. It is, therefore, necessary—at least, wise—to organize the time and activities for the group. So far as is practical, a normal environment should be provided when a team is traveling. If the games are within a short distance of home, a hundred miles or less, and travel is by auto, one should plan to arrive approximately an hour and a half before the game. This eliminates the tiring experience of standing around and waiting and yet provides sufficient time to relax after the trip.

HOME GAMES

Since the most desirable arrangement is usually the normal one, the home-game plans will be presented first. Players should attend all classes as usual, because athletic competition should not be used as an excuse for missing classes. An attitude should be built up within the squad that class assignments always come first. If sports do nothing else they should build habits of responsibility and attention to one's obligations and commitments. This procedure fits into the sports picture also. The players are busy and are following their usual routines. As a consequence, they have no time for worrying about or even giving much thought to the game that day until the squad meets for that purpose.

If the game is at night (most contests are played in the evening), the players' routine is not interrupted until after classes are over. When classwork is finished, the squad should be assembled for its final briefing. Practices prior to the game have prepared the squad for the plan of attack to be used in this contest. The salient features in the scouting report have been stressed, the defenses and offenses to be used have been practiced, the general strategy to be employed has been rehearsed, and individual assignments have been given to each player. If this pattern has been followed in regular practice, then a recapitulation, conducted at the time practice is usually held, should suffice. This final briefing should not consume more than thirty minutes—less time if possible. Comments and directions should be precise, specific, definite and brief. This meeting is to give the players only the important points that they will use during the game; and if they are to remember them, wordiness must be avoided. The meeting should not be for the purpose of arousing or keying up the players. It is to be for their instruction and for last-minute reminders. Thinking is desired; therefore, arousing the emotions should be avoided.

The pre-game meal is an important one; and if it is to be a

help and not a hindrance to the players, it must be planned in accordance with sound principles of physiology and good health habits. In the first place, one's nervous system is conditioned to respond in accordance with his regular eating habits. Most people eat three meals a day and at more or less the same time each day. Whenever possible, this same regularity should be followed on the day of the game in order not to abuse the nervous system.

If the pre-game meal is eaten at regular mealtime, it will probably be eaten at five or six o'clock or about two hours before the game. This meal, if it is not to be harmful to the individual, must be light, comparatively free of fats, and consisting largely of carbohydrates. It is desirable that the stomach complete its action before the game, and the type of food suggested will be discharged from the stomach within about two hours. Some of its sugars that are digested may be converted into energy that will be useful during the game. Generally speaking, however, the purpose of the meal eaten at this time is to allay the sensation of hunger brought about by the peristaltic action of the stomach muscles that becomes rather violent at mealtime. Some players have a feeling of weakness if they do not eat something at their accustomed time. This type of pre-game meal usually satisfies this feeling.

Whether the pre-game meal is eaten at home, at another regular place of eating, or the squad eats together, arrangements can be made to provide the proper foods. A suggested menu can be given to the parents, who are always eager and willing to cooperate. If the meal is to be at a school dining room, a boarding house, or a fraternity house, arrangements can usually be made. If the squad is eating together, the meal can be ordered as desired. The same is true at a restaurant. In no case should an attempt be made to appease the appetite of boys, because they are always hungry and their appetites are insatiable. They will cooperate and are usually satisfied when the procedure is explained to them and they realize that it is in their own interests.

A suggested menu for a pre-game meal, eaten two hours before a game, is as follows:

2 soft poached eggs
dry toast (maximum of 4 slices)
peaches or pears in deep syrup
honey
very weak tea

Some boys do not like eggs so these may be omitted under such circumstances. It will be noted that this meal consists largely of sugar. Honey is a near-perfect form of sugar and is very easily and quickly converted into usable energy. Deep syrup is recommended because it has a heavy concentration of sugar.

Many coaches feel that their players must have a very substantial meal and that a steak is necessary if they are to maintain their strength throughout the game. There is, of course, no validity to such a belief. Some of the greatest feats of endurance and strength have been performed by those who do not eat any meat. If, however, a heavy meal is desired, it should be eaten at least four hours prior to the game. This is to give the stomach time to do its work and to empty before the strenuous effort and emotional stress incident to the game. According to Steinhaus,[1] digestion is retarded under extreme emotional stress. Food retained in the stomach under these circumstances can cause nausea and is likely to reduce one's playing effectiveness.

For heavier meals, no specific menu is suggested. Some general principles may be helpful in ordering meals for the squad and in making suggestions to the players or their parents if the squad is not eating together:

1. Boiled, broiled, and baked foods are always better from a digestive point of view. Foods prepared in this manner have much less fat than fried foods; and, of course, fat is the slowest and most difficult food to digest. The body does not require as large an amount of fat as it does carbohydrates and proteins.

---

[1] Arthur Steinhaus, "Physiology at the Service of Physical Education," *Junior Health and Physical Education,* III, No. 2 (February 1932) and II, Nos. 1 & 2 (January 1931).

2. Some coaches do not permit their players to drink milk during their pre-game meal. They think that it causes "cotton" mouth or dry mouth, or forms thick saliva which is uncomfortable to the player and makes breathing difficult. There is no evidence to support such a theory. Athletes at all times are bothered by these conditions, but so far as is known the cause is nervousness and not food. Milk is an excellent food. Its use should be encouraged rather than discouraged.

3. The principal concern of the coach should be to provide a balanced diet for his players in quantities that are in keeping with the energy requirements of the activity. Variety is desirable for appeal to the appetite.

Some years ago, Dr. Walter Brown, a noted health educator, was asked to make recommendations for a diet for athletes. His recommendations are physiologically sound today. They are repeated here as a sound guide for each coach to follow:

> 1 quart of milk
> 2 servings of fruit—one fresh
> rye, corn, or wholewheat bread
> 3 vegetables—one must be served raw, as in a salad; one
>   should be leafy; and one should be of the root family
> potatoes
> butter—three pats
> eggs—two; alone or in some food
> meat (beef or lamb recommended) or fish once daily
> whole-wheat cereal once daily.

4. Digestion takes place best in a happy, pleasant, relaxed atmosphere; so every effort should be made by the coach to create this kind of an environment for his players during mealtime. This is no time to talk shop.

Some players are so nervous before a game that they are unable to eat anything. Eating may make some nauseated. For this reason, no player should be forced to eat. If he is in good condition, he will not need the energy from the pre-game meal for the immediate contest. Much of that energy will not be available anyway.

In the matter of diet and eating habits, the coach, through the example and pattern that he sets for his players, can create a most valuable influence that may have lifelong effect. It can contribute to the sum total of the healthful living habits of his boys. These tangential aspects of the game thus become important, even vital, concomitants.

Following the pre-game meal, a period of rest is recommended. Sleep, complete rest, is not necessary; but an hour or two off the feet right after a substantial meal will conserve energy and aid digestion. It may even relax jangled nerves.

The squad should report to the dressing room about one hour before game time. This gives plenty of time for taping and for dressing leisurely.

Final instructions are desirable before the team goes on the floor for its warmup. No more than ten or fifteen minutes should be used for a short recapitulation of game plans and strategy and for the final mental preparation of the players (many times a "pat" or a "slap"). When the players go onto the court, they should be ready to play. In basketball, players can get too tense for good performance. However any emotional tenseness will usually wear off during the fifteen- to twenty-minute warmup. For this reason, bringing a squad back to the dressing room after the final pre-game session can do more harm than good. Better results can be accomplished by going to individuals during the warmup with additional advice, directions, or encouragement, and by pointing out opponents and some of their idiosyncrasies than by creating a pressure scene by bringing the whole squad back to the dressing room.

The warmup should not be too strenuous. Too much intense jumping may adversely affect jumping efforts during the game because a muscle under extreme stretch tires rapidly.[2] The purpose of the warmup is to prepare the circulation so that a player may reach his steady state and thus be able to start off the game at his normal rate without distress and maintain this rate

---

2 John W. Bunn, *Scientific Principles of Coaching* (Englewood Cliffs, N.J.: Prentice-Hall, Inc., 1955), p. 90.

throughout the game. For this reason, considerable running is desirable. Also, the players need some shooting practice at their favorite spots as well as with varied shots in order to adjust to court conditions.

GAMES AWAY FROM HOME

When the team is traveling, the normal conditions of living are disturbed. Much leisure time is at the disposal of the players. Eating schedules are often upset. A strange environment is produced. For these reasons, it is desirable to set up a plan of action for the squad.

If the squad is traveling during school time, it is desirable to encourage the players to take school assignments with them so that they will not fall behind in their classwork. More time will be available for study on a trip than when the players are at home, so that much can be accomplished on a trip if the players will invest their time profitably.

Standing around in hotel lobbies or walking the streets can be very wearying. All running about should be planned for the mornings. Long walks, visiting the campus of the host's school, and limited sightseeing should be confined to the forenoon. The afternoon should be spent in the room studying or resting. In any event, the players should be asked to stay off their feet as much as possible. This routine and the rest following the pre-game meal will prepare the boys for their evening game.

Some of the time can be invested profitably in discussing basketball, a review of the opponent's tactics, an analysis of the previous night's game (when more than one game is scheduled on a trip), rules discussion, and strategy sessions. These can be carried out in an informal fashion with the squad participating and not just listening. The use of a magnetic board (Red Rolfe, who was as much of a basketball student as he was a Yankee third baseman, always carried a cardboard court and checkers with him for setting up play situations for discussion and analysis) can be enjoyable as well as helpful.

When boys have nothing to do or are sitting about idly, they want to eat. Digestive upsets can result; and when these occur, playing efficiency usually drops. Also, undesirable health habits are being established. One need not fear that boys do not get enough food. Most overeat. They permit appetite to dictate their eating habits. For these reasons, eating schedules should be carefully controlled.

A schedule that fits ideally the many unnatural situations created by traveling, even though it departs from the normal eating schedule which is maintained at home, is to have break-fast at ten o'clock, the pre-game meal at four (when game is to be played at eight or eight-thirty) and a snack after the game. By following this schedule, the usual three-meals-a-day routine is followed; the main meal is eaten at least four hours before game time; and a light snack will not interfere with sleep if eaten after the game.

This schedule tends to cut down the desire to eat between meals. By delaying breakfast until ten o'clock, the boys are permitted to sleep late if they desire; and most like this idea. When more than one game is played, it is usually difficult for them to get to bed early after a game; so by sleeping late, they obtain sufficient rest. After a game, it takes some time to relax so that sleep is possible. A *light* snack an hour or so after the game may help to relax the group. For this snack, fruit, a warm drink such as hot chocolate, and chicken à la king or creamed tuna are suggested.

The snack after the game also affords an excuse to get the squad together, whether in victory or defeat. If the game was lost, the boys may need to be cheered up; morale problems can often be handled automatically by such a gathering. If the game was won, the gathering affords an opportunity to celebrate. Win or lose, it is a chance to talk over the game informally.

Many coaches follow the plan of giving money to their players and permitting them to eat on their own. By following this practice, a golden opportunity to develop a team spirit and a oneness of purpose is lost. It also affords an opportunity for cliques to form—at least it encourages it. For this reason, the squad should always eat together as a family when traveling; and the coach should always eat with his boys. On trips the coach and team have time to get intimately acquainted. Sometimes the best job of coaching can be done during such periods. If the squad is permitted to separate, to go visiting, and to be guests of others at mealtime, not only are these opportunities lost but, many times, intersquad problems develop.

PRACTICE ON DAY OF GAME

The problem of whether to practice or not on the day of a game is one that provokes many and varied opinions. Reference here is made to the traveling team. So far as is known, there is no tangible guide that a coach may follow. Does a team benefit from such practice? There is probably no clear-cut answer. Teams have sometimes played well and sometimes played poorly after a practice on the day of a game and vice versa. However, it is not known whether the practice or the lack of it had any relation to the caliber of performance.

One might ask the purpose of practice the day of a game. Certainly it is not needed for exercise. On the other hand, this practice, if not carried on intensely or to the point of extreme fatigue, will probably have no deleterious effect on physical condition or on the resulting play during the game. If players were at home, it is possible that in many instances they would be carrying on physical activity which is more enervating than a light practice.

Most coaches at some time have held or do hold practice on the day of a game when traveling. Why and under what circumstances do they schedule such practices? Undoubtedly, some do it because that is what their coach did; he was successful, so it is a tradition. This kind of reasoning does not stand up favorably to critical analysis. It is possible that a team is successful in spite of such practices.

The following is an attempt to analyze this problem in terms of the situation that may prevail and in terms of the players. By studying these points and then relating them to his team and to the situation at the moment, a coach can determine on each occasion what seems to be the best procedure for his team. The implication here is that there may be occasions where a light practice is indicated and other occasions when no practice at all seems best.

1. A light practice on the day of a game may be used as a means of occupying the time of the players on a trip. It reduces the amount of idle waiting time and removes players from the tiresome practice of standing around.

If this is the primary reason for practice, a short, brisk walk may be organized for the squad; thereafter, they may be asked to avoid standing around and to devote themselves to their schoolwork.

2. A light practice may be used to familiarize the squad with its playing surroundings on a strange court. Where conditions—size of court, light intensity, rigidity of the back boards, ceiling height, and background—vary extremely from those of one's home court, there is some logic in holding a light practice. It permits players to make adjustments in their perspective in shooting and in many cases it permits an opportunity for players to make them in advance. Practicing, first, on a small court with a low ceiling, with the wall at the end close to the end line, and with the backboards attached to a balcony, and then traveling to a facility comparable to Madison Square Garden in New York can create an emotional problem that is reflected in performance. Under such conditions, some practice may be desirable.

3. A light practice after a long, tiresome trip accompanied by comparative physical inactivity can have favorable therapeutic effects. There is much evidence to commend a period of exercise after a strenuous day at the office as a refresher for the mind and body. Confinement on a train, in a car, or on a plane can be just as tiring as a strenuous day in the office. If per-

chance, the time schedule permits this refresher the day before, the need for it on the day of the game is removed.

4. If the program of practice and play of a team has been intense, continuous, and it has been conducted under extreme pressure for a long period, freedom and relief from practice of any kind is decidedly more beneficial than even a light practice. There is ample evidence to support this position. It is the justification for a vacation. The maintenance of continued routine and regimentation creates diminishing returns in all walks of life. Industry has found that increased production is maintained by regularly scheduled rest periods; the incidence of accidents is reduced. The problem of physical fatigue is not as important here as mental fatigue. Justification for a vacation is based upon this experience.

Many coaches feel that they must work their players continually to attain perfection. This feeling persists more strongly if a team is playing poorly. But following this philosophy frequently brings the onset of diminishing returns and just the opposite effect from that desired. Resumption of practice after a break in the routine is by far more productive. One must also take into consideration the law of maturation and plateaus of learning wherein the necessity for a lapse in activity to permit growth is implicit.

5. After a long layoff (during a vacation or examination period), a short period of practice to regain one's "touch" can be beneficial. In this connection, it may be desirable to conduct short practices for the reserve players, those who are not playing regularly. In this way, they are able to substitute partially for their lack of activity.

On the basis of the above, it is the job of the coach to make his own evaluations and act accordingly. In view of the general tendency to overemphasize, it is probably wise to follow a general policy of no practice and then to make the few exceptions where it seems to be necessary. In this way, the game is not likely to be played prior to the actual contest.

16

BETWEEN HALVES

What should a coach do with his team between halves? There probably is no stock answer. So much depends upon the individual characteristics of the players; on the game situation at half-time; on how each player is performing during this game (his scoring, his fouls, his poise, his defense); on the performance of the team as a whole; on how the opponents are performing and their poise or lack of it; on the general characteristics of the opponents; and on the plan of play previously determined for this particular game. All these or any one of them should form the basis for specific between-halves procedure. The ability of the coach to evaluate the over-all situation accurately will determine his subsequent moves.

Whatever he does should be specific and constructive. To chide a team for not scoring more is neither specific nor constructive. When a coach was overheard to use this approach on one occasion, a player was heard to ask, "Well, coach, why haven't we scored any more?"—a proper rejoinder to such a tirade. The players need a positive analysis of their play. It is the purpose of this chapter to present and discuss general principles for guiding the coach in his relations with his team and then to give examples of intermission activities which on the basis of analysis of the first-half play have turned out favorably.

Three words may be used to describe the sequence of action between halves—Revive! Advise! Drive!

THE REVIVAL PERIOD

Unless there is evidence of some friction between players because of something that has occurred during the first half, it is wise to permit them to have the first few minutes of the intermission to themselves. They will relax easier and it gives them an uninhibited opportunity to analyze the first-half play. This procedure often proves more valuable than if the coach dominates the scene. The coach can spend these few minutes most profitably in checking the scorebook and the shot and rebound charts. He may sit on the bench and uninterruptedly analyze the first-half play and determine second-half strategy. If he has assistants, he can go quickly over plans with them and receive advice from them.

Before the game, the players can be directed concerning any routine procedures which they are to follow between halves. The manager and trainer can always be helpful in assisting the players before the coach comes into the dressing room. Players will be refreshed if they will wipe their faces with a cold, moist towel. There is no valid reason to deprive them of a drink of water, because water tends to replace the moisture lost through perspiration. Excessive drinking should, of course, be avoided. The custom of sucking oranges provides a very small amount of sugar which may be useful during the second half. It also helps to relieve the dry-cotton mouth caused by nervousness. If players can stretch out, they rest more readily. Ventilation, without draft, is of course desirable.

If the coach does go into the dressing room as his squad enters, he should address himself, with few exceptions, to the task of looking after the individual needs of each player.

In addition to the common practices for revival during the intermission, recent research [1] has shown the value of cold packs in helping players to exceed, during the second half, their performance of the first half. For this purpose, ice bags may be placed on the abdomen and kept there from the time the players enter the dressing room at intermission until they go back on the court for the second half.

The effect of ice packs is to facilitate recovery from fatigue. They decrease the basal metabolism of the body more rapidly than is caused by a decrease in body temperature. Less oxygen is required and the pulse rate is reduced; and ice packs have removed nausea.

Subjects have performed on the ergometer, have done the Carlson Spot Run, and have run a 440-yard dash. After their first test, they would rest before the second test with and without ice packs. In all cases where the rest period was without ice packs, there was no improvement in performance. When ice packs were used during the rest period, there was always significant improvement in performance.

On the above basis, ice packs are strongly recommended as an aid in recovery between halves. Once players become accustomed to the shock of a cold pack on the warm abdomen, they invariably become enthusiastic about its use; but the use of ice packs should not be made mandatory. Invariably, the players have chosen to use them after preliminary experimentation. They have even been used with refreshing effect during the second half while a player was sitting on the bench after being withdrawn from the game temporarily.

During the revival period some players may need the attention of the trainer for such things as changing bandages and adjusting taping.

---

[1] Robert Alpert, "Influence of Cold Abdominal Pack on Carlson Fatigue Tests" (Master's thesis, University of Iowa, 1952); and William Happ, "Physiological Effects of Cold Abdominal Pack" (Master's thesis, University of Iowa, 1948.)

THE ADVICE PERIOD

The next five to seven minutes (three if a high school game) should be spent in preparing the team for the plan of play for the second half. Whereas during the revival period there may be talking, discussions, moving about of players, managers, and trainer, during the period of advising the coach must have the undivided attention of everyone in the room. Players may ask questions or make comments on the coach's directions, but everything must be pointed toward the strategy for the second half.

The procedure during this period should be first, to give suggestions and encouragement to individuals, and then to give directions for team play. Next, defense, then offense, and finally the plan for getting the ball on the tip-off at the opening of the second half are dealt with. Included in these remarks should be a prognostication of what may be expected from the opponents and how to meet it.

Generally speaking, these instructions should be presented without too much animation. Clear, collected thinking is desired. Usually basketball players can be keyed to too high a pitch for their own good. To aggravate tension is to destroy effectiveness.

It is much more effective to select what seem to the coach to be the most pertinent points, than to attempt to point out every detail. Three or four points clearly and concisely presented, remembered and executed are more effective than twelve points confused and forgotten when the directions are completed. There may be times when there is little or nothing to say except for encouragement. There is greater danger in saying too much than in saying too little.

Specific Half-time Procedures

The recitation of a few actual half-time procedures may be helpful:

1. A striking example of the good results of keeping still is shown in the story told about Jim Baggott, the Greeley, Colorado, high school coach whose teams have a habit of participating in the state tournament each year. During the finals one year his small team came out for the second half and literally ran a giant opponent off the court. After the game, one of his pint-sized players was asked, "What did Coach say to you during intermission that made you fellows play like demons during the second half?" The answer was "Nothing." When Jim was asked about the statement, he said, "There was no need to say anything. We had worked out our strategy before the game and the game was going according to plan. The kids knew what they were going to do during the second half. They were so eager to get back on the court and get going that my job was to keep them quiet until the intermission was over."

2. Several years ago a certain team had played very poorly during the first half. They had not done anything according to plan. The team appeared listless, even sluggish. It was apparent that some heroic methods were needed if the team was to prevent a first-half deficit of twenty points from becoming a rout. Time might have been spent uselessly in pointing out all of the errors to be corrected during the second half. Instead the coach started to make some suggestions and then in a fit of feigned anger, said, "Oh, what's the use? You fellows wouldn't follow instructions if they were typed in bold-faced letters and handed to you on cards. You're not the team tonight with which a coach is proud to be associated. You seem to be playing according to your own plan, whatever that is, so maybe you can work out your own solution." With that he stalked out of the dressing room and sat in the stands during the second half while his assistant sat with the team. The play of the team was a revelation. It overcame a margin of twenty points and won in the last few minutes of the game. The coach went into the dressing room after the game to congratulate his boys and to say that they were the kind of boys in the second half that he was proud to claim.

They informed him in jest that they were planning a meeting to decide whether or not they would let him join them again.

3. In another game, a team was playing well and with great spirit but all the breaks seemed to be going against it, so that at the end of the half it was behind seventeen points. All the coach did between halves was to speak words of encouragement and to joke with the players in order to relax them. He said, "I wouldn't know how to tell you to play this game any differently. Surely the breaks can't continue to go against you the whole game." With this vote of confidence the team overcame its opponent in the last second of play and won by one point.

4. In a Christmas tournament one year, a team was playing only mediocre ball. In particular, it was unable to stop the scoring of one opponent who had collected twenty points at half-time. It was decided at half-time to press this team for the whole second half and to assign one man to the high scorer. These were all the instructions given. The strategy worked. The high scorer was held without a field goal in the second half. The opponent who had played flawlessly during the first half became erratic because of the press and was easily beaten.

It should be stated here that a change in game strategy should include only those plans of play in which the team has been drilled. It is expecting the impossible to think that a team can change its habits of play by wishful thinking or imagining it is adept where it is not.

The foregoing examples have all recounted situations where a team has been behind at the half. What is the procedure when a team is ahead? Many coaches feel that it is much easier to prescribe when a team is behind or not playing well. They even prefer to be a few points behind at the half because they feel that the mental attitude of their players will be better to start the second half and that players can be motivated more effectively because there is a greater challenge when they are behind. Undoubtedly, there is some logic to these points but it is doubted if a coach deliberately plans a game or directs his team to play so it will be behind at the half. Except when the score is tied, of course, one team is ahead at the half. Consequently the coach must be prepared to plan the second half under these conditions.

Several specific guides can be suggested:

1. When a team is ahead at the half—particularly if it is far ahead—the coach should alert his team to the possible type of play to expect from the opponent during the second half. This can be done with considerable accuracy if the philosophy of the coach of the opponent is known and if the characteristics of play of the opposing team are known through scouting reports. In general, the play of teams follows a definite pattern and cannot be successfully changed overnight. In a similar manner, the strategy of coaches follows a rather consistent pattern; so it pays to study the coach.

2. If the plan of play for the game at hand has developed according to prediction through the first half, then, generally speaking, it will be wise to continue according to previously devised plans for the second half.

3. The coach must always be sensitive to any evidences of a self-satisfied attitude. This should not be confused with an air of confidence which is always desirable and should be encouraged. A self-satisfied attitude begets lethargy and carelessness. It can usually be handled directly by pointing out some of the errors in the first-half play or indirectly by concentrating attention on some specific phase of the plan for second-half play.

4. There are many occasions when the coach should commend his team enthusiastically on its sterling performance, with the confident expectation that they will do even better the second half. This approach is particularly desirable with a developing, hustling team of youngsters who lack experience.

THE DRIVE PERIOD

The third phase of the between-half procedure, the drive phase, affords the coach the opportunity for a bit of psychological coaching as a parting shot just before players return to the court. It's the climax of the intermission. Many coaches do not believe in this aspect of coaching. However, anyone familiar with the principles of psychology realizes that with the proper mental stimulus players may be stirred to superhuman feats. The art of selecting the correct tactic is contingent upon the understanding of one's players and the ability to analyze the group correctly at a particular moment.

Some of the examples of procedures during the "Advice" period can be used during the "Drive" phase. A group of sensitive, overly conscientious boys must be handled with much greater care than a lethargic, callous team. A seasoned, senior team can be treated more sternly than an inexperienced team still lacking confidence.

The term "drive" may be a bit misleading unless the full connotation of the term is indicated. A "wisecrack" to relieve tension when a team is noticeably nervous and too keyed up may be just the right touch. A verbal pat on the back can be tremendously stimulating. An expression of faith and confidence may be just the tonic a group needs. These methods are all just as much a part of the "Drive" phase of intermission as are the dramatic efforts of a coach to arouse his team to just the right emotional state that will impel it to superhuman performances.

17

STORIES WITH
A PURPOSE

Basketball stories are legion, and many are very amusing. Those related here represent incidents in the experience of the author with his boys. Most of them are related to game situations and the reactions of players under intense conditions. In this respect they have tremendous implications for the coach in that they point to procedures for influencing behavior patterns of players toward more effective performance. It is for this reason that they are presented.

THE "LAUGHING BOYS" OF
MADISON SQUARE GARDEN

It seems a paradox to say that basketball is both an intense game and one in which boys must be relaxed to perform at their best. However, this is literally true.

The fabulous Stanford University basketball team of the 1930's traveled east to make its debut against Clair Bee's Long Island University team, which was undefeated in forty-three games. The overflow crowd in Madison Square Garden, to say nothing of the veteran Long Island team, was enough to bewilder any bunch of green sophomores.

As this crucial game got under way, it was evident to all that the Stanford team was taut. Their shooting was erratic. They fumbled the ball and made many bad passes. Fortunately, the score continued about even for twelve minutes in the first half. At this point, an incident occurred that changed the whole complexion of the game and the outcome.

Howie Turner, the handsome, rosy-cheeked cherub of the Indians, cut across the free-throw circle from the side of the court to receive a bounce pass from Hank Luisetti. The pass was almost out of reach. In stretching to catch the ball, Howie lost his balance. He was at the point of running with it. As he fell to the floor, he heaved the ball into the air and scrambled to his feet to get back on defense. As he reached the center of the court, he turned to look toward his own basket. No one was running and the referee was retrieving the ball to return it to the center circle for a jump ball (this was before the elimination of the center jump).

Howie seemed unable to comprehend the situation. He pointed to the basket and in pantomime asked if the heave which he made had scored a goal. When told that it had, he covered his eyes, shook his head, and then broke into a hilarious laugh. His mirth was infectious, and his teammates soon shook with laughter; the huge crowd joined in the spirit of the ridiculous fluke. Only the L.I.U. team failed to see the humor in the occasion.

This accidental incident had the needed relaxing effect on the Stanford boys. They scored twelve straight points thereafter before L.I.U. could again get into the scoring column. As a result of this incident, a close, hectic contest was turned into a rout. The Stanford team thereafter was labeled the "Laughing Boys," a monicker that stuck with them throughout their career.

A NEEDED MOMENT OF RELIEF

At one time, the Pacific Coast Conference was divided into the North and South for purposes of basketball competition; and at the end of the regular playing season the champion of the

North played the champion of the South to determine the champion of the conference.

On one occasion, Stanford was the winner in the South and the University of Washington was the winner in the North. The two teams were to meet in their first play-off game in the Civic Auditorium in San Francisco.

In pre-season competition, Washington had defeated Stanford twice by rather large margins. As a consequence, the Stanford squad was very apprehensive about the outcome of the championship series. Instead of the usual good humor and joviality at the pre-game meal, there was an ominous tenseness and irritability—certainly not a favorable atmosphere for good digestion or for entering into a championship game.

Sensing the situation, the coach attempted by kidding, jokes, and diverting conversation to relieve the tension; but all efforts were to no avail. Jokes fell on unreceptive ears, and other attempts at conversation met with disgusted looks. Then the inevitable happened.

Dinty Moore, the team captain and the irrepressible good-humor boy, loved by all his teammates, saved the day. He was tardy in reporting for the pre-game meal. When he arrived, instead of going to his seat at the table, he walked over and stood behind the chair of Hank Luisetti, the three-time All-American. No one paid attention to him until he chanted in a falsetto voice: "I'll see you tomorrow night after the game, Eleanor."

There was a moment's silence, then pandemonium broke loose. A sheepish, embarrassed grin spread over Hank's face. His face and neck turned red. His eyes moved from one face to another about the table. When his gaze fell upon Phil Zonne, a sophomore forward and a fraternity brother, he jumped to his feet with, "Damn you, Zonne," and tore around the table with Phil in headlong flight. Hank had been overheard uttering, in honeyed tones, the quoted parting words as he talked with his girl the night before.

Everyone forgot the game for a moment. The needed relief incident had occurred, and all enjoyed the good-natured scuffle which followed. Needless to say, the team went onto the floor fully relaxed, and they defeated Washington by more than twenty points. Luisetti played one of the greatest games of his great career. This is just another example of the value of relaxation and of how incidents can accrue to the benefit of a team. It pays to develop the spirit of fun within a squad.

DIVERTING ATTENTION
FROM A FEARED OPPONENT

When the colorful, bombastic Frank Keaney was coaching basketball and teaching chemistry at Rhode Island University, his teams were the scourge of the east. His was a wide-open game. He had the "runningest," "shootingest" teams that could be found anywhere. His players were never large but they were fast and tricky, and they could hold their own with the best.

It was said that there was no organization to his play. It was helter-skelter and, therefore, no special defense could be planned. When the writer went to Springfield College, he found that Rhode Island University was on the basketball schedule. The Rhode Island team was scouted several times with the hope of finding some clue to the strategy and plan of play used by this team. Contrary to reports, it was discovered that while this team played a wide-open game, there was as much planning and as definite organization to its play as if it were a mechanical, ball-control team.

The Springfield team did not share this belief and as the date of the game drew nearer it was evident that something heroic needed to be done to reassure the Springfield boys, to allay their fears, and to give them a modicum of confidence.

Springfield students were not wealthy, and many were not able to eat as heartily as they would have liked. Certainly this was true of the basketball players. This fact was capitalized upon with the hope of using it in preparation for the coming game.

In order to emphasize dramatically the opinion that Rhode

Island basketball was as definitely organized as any other, this statement was made: "Boys, the Rhode Island team has been scouted four times. The consensus regarding the reports is that the Rhode Island University basketball team is as decidedly organized as any other team in the country." They were then shown by diagrams the methods of play. Then this added emphasis was given: "The team is even stereotyped in its pattern of play. This is so definite that the spot to which the ball will be tipped at the opening tip-off is known. This is believed so strongly that if the ball does not go to this spot, every one of you will be treated to the best dinner that can be bought downtown."

This last statement did the trick. Rhode Island was of secondary importance to those hungry warriors. Their interest was now intense, and their fears were gone. As they licked their chops in anticipation of a full meal, the question from each was, "All right, coach, where will they tip the ball?" When the tip-off was diagrammed, their next question was, "Do you really mean your offer and does it include the whole squad?" When reassured, they could hardly wait for the tip-off.

On the following evening as the teams lined up to start the game, never before had there been so much eagerness on the bench and on the floor. The ball was tossed. Rhode Island's center controlled the tip—no, the ball didn't go to the designated spot, but the Springfield captain, John Burke, recovered it. The bench cheered as if the game had ended and a victory had been won. Fourteen hungry, jubilant eyes looked intently at the coach.

The Springfield captain dribbled the ball toward his team's bench. As he drew alongside, a broad smile framed his face as he challenged, "Remember what you said, coach!" The answer was, "I'll make good on my part of the bargain. Now you boys do your stuff."

It was a terrific game, with Springfield pulling comfortably ahead at the end for the first time in the era of Frank Keaney. The players enjoyed a full meal.

PRE-GAME INSTRUCTIONS

Probably every coach takes a few minutes prior to sending his team on the floor to review the game plan which is to be followed. For an important intersectional game, rather specific and complete scouting notes had been received. These had been reviewed several times with the squad so that everyone was very familiar with the strategy for the game. The coach was approaching the team's dressing room to send his squad onto the floor. The door was slightly ajar so that he could hear someone marching back and forth before the squad repeating, in the coach's way of speaking, all the details which had been covered for this game. The coach stopped outside and listened until the talk was completed and the squad was despatched, figuratively, to the court. They clapped and yelled at this point and just then the coach appeared in the doorway. A quiet embarrassment prevailed because no one could be sure that the coach had heard or how he would react until he said, with a smile, "It seems to me that you have your complete instructions, so let's go." Then everyone broke into good-natured laughter and ran out for the pre-game warmup. It is needless to conclude that the team turned in a great performance.

THE SUBTLE DISCIPLINARIAN

Dr. F. C. Allen will be remembered in basketball as one of the greatest leaders and uncanniest diagnosticians of all time. He had great insight. He understood boys and knew how to handle them, to get the most in performance from them. These qualities were probably his greatest assets as a coach. It was the author's privilege to play for him and then to assist him for ten years at the University of Kansas.

During this association, many situations arose which revealed the uncanny ability of "Phog" to demonstrate his genius. One situation in particular has left an indelible impression on me.

For some reason unknown to me, the Kansas team in one season was not developing into the smooth combination or the spirited "gang" so characteristic of Allen-coached teams.

The caliber of players seemed to be up to standard, but they were not melding into a satisfactory unit. The team was not an inexperienced one. Four players were regulars from the year before. The one who apparently had won fifth place on the team was a sophomore. He was a talented youngster, the outstanding player on the freshman squad from the year before. However, for some reason or other, the others did not play well when this boy was in the line-up. Neither did the team play effectively as a whole.

It was drawing near to the time for the first game of the season. I was beginning to worry for fear that "Doc" had not picked the right combination. Finally, when the first game was less than two weeks away, I was called into Dr. Allen's office. When I entered, the four veterans from the previous year were sitting in the office. As I sat down, "Doc" opened the meeting as follows:

"Boys, I have asked you to come in because each of you has come to me independently and, I am sure, unaware that the others have talked to me during the past week with essentially the same concern. Each of you recognizes the sterling basketball qualities in ———— (we'll call him Harry—the sophomore). But each of you has felt a lack of coordinated effort when Harry is in the line-up. And each of you shares the same concern with me as the opening of the season draws near. Likewise, each of you seems to be unable to diagnose the trouble, except that you don't seem to be able to play with him."

"I thought we should all get together to see if we couldn't analyze the difficulty. Do you have anything further to add to the situation?" No further enlightenment was offered.

"You are convinced that you can't play with Harry?" Regretfully they were.

Then came the bombshell that revealed to me the uncanny shrewdness of the man.

"Well, since you fellows are sure that it will be necessary to find a different combination, I thought it only fair to let you know in advance that the one person who is set in the line-up is Harry. I had hoped that you four would gradually begin to work smoothly with him. But if, as you say, you are convinced that this, for some unaccountable reason, seems impossible, it will be necessary for me to start a frantic search for another combination. I hate to do this because the time is so short.

"Before I make the move I suggest, while I am weighing the other possibilities, that we work together a couple more days. Now that we understand each other, it may be that by united effort we can smooth out our play. Are you willing to try for a couple more days?"

It is needless to say they were. And with that agreement, the meeting broke up. Phog called me back for a moment and when the players had left, he asked, "Do you know the trouble?" I had no idea. He then enlightened me. A clique had been developing in the squad. The four veterans had decided that one of their gang should be playing instead of Harry, who was not one of them. Phog had sensed the situation and made the above surprise-move to break it up. The veterans were, of course, taken aback by this turn of events. They had never dreamed of action like this. But they knew their coach well enough to realize that even if he were bluffing he would carry out any plans that were announced as definitely as these.

Subsequent practices were a joy to watch. The veterans found out that Harry did fit into the line-up after all and Kansas opened the season in a fashion that heralded another powerful Jayhawker combination.

BEHIND FORTY MINUTES— BUT A WINNER

The Springfield College team of 1953 hit its stride at mid-season. It was on a trip into Vermont to finish its season with games against Middlebury and Norwich. Springfield was protecting a nine-game winning streak, but it approached the Middlebury game with considerable uneasiness, because the opponent had a much better team than its record indicated. It was fast and well balanced. This was its final game of the season and the players agreed during the warmup period that they were determined to finish their season with a victory.

A few minutes after the opening of the game, it became evident that they would likely achieve their goal. Springfield played one of its better games but was never ahead during the first half. The half ended with Springfield trailing by nine points.

Between halves the players did not need to be reminded of their problem. If anything, they sensed it too keenly. They were so keyed up that it was not possible to quiet them during intermission. Fortunately, the time keeper (he was destined to err again) allowed only ten minutes between halves so the players were relieved of the agony of waiting the full fifteen minutes.

The second half was a repetition of the first. At one time in the third quarter, Springfield trailed by twenty-five points. Midway in the third quarter a full-court press was ordered. The lead was reduced somewhat but with two minutes and eighteen seconds left, Middlebury led by eleven points.

Chances for a Springfield victory looked hopeless. The packed Middlebury fieldhouse reflected the air of victory. Some of the more confident started to leave to avoid the traffic rush after the game. And then it happened! In a superhuman effort, Springfield intercepted the ball five times; and five times a different player scored without a single return by Middlebury.

Now the crowd was tense, but still confident of Middlebury's victory. Only fifteen seconds remained to play. Middlebury had the ball out of bounds for the throw-in after the fifth basket. The Springfield players were desperate. Playing five against four, they forced a long pass on the throw-in. The pass was wild. The ball was touched by a Middlebury player but not controlled. It went out of bounds at mid-court where it was awarded to Springfield.

The Springfield captain called time-out. The request was

granted but the timer failed to stop the clock. Seven precious seconds were ticked away before the assistant coach, Ed Steitz, who rushed to the timer's table, could get the clock stopped. Two seconds remained. The officials had no basis for changing the time in spite of protests, so the playing time remained at two seconds as indicated on the clock.

Springfield had used only two of its five time-outs, so took the remaining three in succession in order to plan a play that would give a shot with a reasonable chance to score.

With the ball at mid-court, two seconds remained to be played. Remembering that the clock starts as soon as the ball is touched on the floor, assistant coach Ed Steitz concocted the following play. A boy with a strong throwing arm was directed to take the ball out of bounds and to throw it as hard as possible and aim at the backboard. The best rebounder on the team, Al Schutts, was placed in rebound position. For added insurance, little Bobby Morrison, a substitute guard who became captain the next year, was placed ten feet behind Schutts for the purpose of getting the ball and the shot in case the throw-in went wild or Schutts was blocked out. The two other players were placed at the mid-line but in the front court to criss-cross for the purpose of setting up diversionary action.

The play was explained to the officials. They were asked to instruct the timer not to start the clock until the ball was actually touched after the throw-in so that a third error would be avoided.

The stage was set. The crowd was tense, absolutely quiet, not quite so sure of victory now and yet doubtful that a score could result in two seconds. Middlebury sensed the play, so effectively blocked Schutts from the goal. The throw-in hit the backboard high, rebounded above the reach of the players swarming the goal. It hit the floor between Schutts and Morrison and bounded high in the air. Morrison rushed toward the ball, jumped into the air to catch it, and shot quickly while he was still in the air. The shot was from the side and about fifteen feet from the goal. The ball had barely left Morrison's hand when the gun fired to end the game. The shot was perfect. The ball touched nothing but the bottom of the net as it flicked through the basket.

Springfield had won by one point, after being behind for the full forty minutes of play. For a moment there was dead silence. Then the Springfield players realized that the impossible had happened. Pandemonium broke loose. They carried Morrison from the court on their shoulders while the Middlebury crowd and players watched in stunned silence, unable to believe what they had seen.

When the team returned to the hotel, one of the guests there who had left the game early when he was sure that Middlebury would win offered his condolences to the boys. He would not believe them when they assured him that they had won. Nothing would convince him until he read the account of the game in the paper the next morning.

Springfield went on to finish a perfect second half of the season.

COUNT THREE

One season, I had a boy who was an excellent rebounder. He had a knack of getting into the right position at the right time to control the ball as it rebounded from the backboard. However, he was so erratic that after getting the ball he threw it away in his haste to pass out for a fast break. Hoping to slow up his action in the interest of greater accuracy, I suggested that after he rebounded and came to the floor with the ball he count three before passing it. This would give him time to form a better judgment and to look before he passed.

In the very next scrimmage, after his first rebound, everyone heard him count three slowly. He then drew back and threw the ball up into the bleachers. This caused so much hilarity that it practically broke up the practice.

HOLIDAY ENTERTAINMENT

E. C. Quigley was probably the greatest official the game of basketball has ever known. Officiating was his business. He was a national league baseball umpire and at one time was chief of the national league umpires. In the fall he refereed football games. In his prime, he worked in most of the important games of the country.

He was a fearless arbiter, fair and fully in control of the game at all times. He had the confidence of players, coaches, and spectators alike. No one ever dared question his decisions. He was the law. Many times he departed from the rules if in his mind justice required that he make his own rules. This partial independence, his dramatic actions on the court, and his powerful booming voice made him a most colorful official.

As my teams traveled through the Middle West (Quigley's home was in St. Mary's, Kansas) during the holiday season, I always asked for Quigley to officiate. On these occasions, several amusing incidents occurred which furnished great merriment to my players.

On one occasion my Stanford team played at the University of Nebraska one night and at Creighton the following night. Quigley was the official in both games. At Lincoln, Quigley had repeatedly called out the name of Stanford as if it were spelled STANF(E)RD. Before the game at Creighton, my little captain, Tommy Cordry, asked if he might correct Mr. Quigley in the pronunciation of the name of our school on the grounds that we were quite sensitive about this point. I saw the amused and mischievous twinkle in his eye so I said, "Yes, providing you make the request in a courteous and gentlemanly fashion."

As Mr. Quigley stepped to the center of the floor preparatory to tossing the ball for the opening toss, Captain Cordry went up to him to make his request. Mr. Quigley listened intently as Cordry spoke soberly and seriously. At the end of the request, Mr. Quigley stepped back away from Captain Cordry and with his arm outstretched and the palm of his hand facing Cordry, said in a voice which could be heard throughout the gym: "Young man, I stand corrected for the first time in my life. Let's play ball."

The Stanford boys roared with laughter. It put them in a relaxed condition to play the game. The crowd, of course, had no idea what had provoked this outburst from Quig, but they were always expecting something from him.

HERO WORSHIP

If one ever doubts the influence of those who are prominent in athletics upon their followers, the following incidents (which could be multiplied endlessly) should serve to remove every shadow of doubt. These two incidents should also serve as a challenge to every boy who competes to set the best possible example in living standards. Someone is likely to emulate him. Surely no one desires deliberately to furnish anything but the best leadership.

One year in the era of Hank Luisetti, Stanford was locked in championship combat with the University of Oregon. In the Stanford Pavilion during the most hectic part of the game, Luisetti made an unbelievable recovery of a wild pass. He dived across the sideline to grab the ball and flicked it backwards to a waiting teammate. As the ball left his hands, he sprawled headlong into the crowd. The action was across the floor from the players' bench. It appeared that someone was hurt. I thought only of the safety of Luisetti. He got back to the court and appeared unharmed. But then Hank, a gentleman under all kinds of stress, instead of returning to play turned his attention to the person who seemed to be injured. He also seemed to be looking for something on the floor. Evidently he found it, because he was seen handing an object to someone on the sideline.

I could not understand the situation and was frantic to know why he didn't get back into the game. Just as he handed something to a spectator, the ball was thrown to him. He caught it deftly with his free hand and with perfect poise and as if there had been no distraction, nonchalantly flipped the ball through the basket twenty-five feet away.

The incident was forgotten, but the next day a small boy crossed my path. He had a cut above his eye and across his nose and there was discoloring about his eye. I asked the boy, jokingly, if he had been in a fight. He replied that he had broken his glasses. When I expressed sympathy, he straightened and with great pride said, "Oh, no, that's all right. Luisetti knocked my glasses off during the game last night. Boy, wasn't he great?"

That's the story of the sideline incident.

The leader of a boys' club in Los Angeles wrote to ask if he could bring his boys around to meet the Stanford team after a game which it was to play soon in Los Angeles. Since the team was to dress at its hotel, it seemed more fitting to invite the boys to come to the hotel and have a snack with the team.

The invitation was accepted. The boys' club group was in the dining room long before the team had arrived. As the team drifted into the dining room by ones and twos, the youngsters were told to introduce themselves. They accepted this idea eagerly. They got autographs and then each picked his favorite player to sit by and to chat with while they all ate.

The hero-worship was evident in the sparkling eyes and eager expressions on the faces of all those youngsters. It was a happy and historic occasion for both the boys and the players.

After the boys left, I was profoundly impressed by the reaction of the players, whose feelings are typified by the following statement that was made by one of the athletes: "I never before realized the tremendous influence we can have on youngsters. This experience has made a lasting impression on me. It shows me the importance of setting an example for good at all times. It would grieve me if I thought I had conducted myself in a manner which was harmful to another."

INDEX